Praise for books by Lar

CHURCHILL Without Blood, Sweat, or Tears

"Both Lincoln and Churchill had their leadership forged in crisis. Larry Kryske's unique leadership perspective reveals Churchill's approach for a new generation of leaders."

Donald T. Phillips
Author of *Lincoln on Leadership for Today*

"Commander Kryske is the right person to share the leadership of Winston Churchill. He demonstrated great leadership, professionalism, and dedication throughout his naval career."

Gene Taylor, Congressman,
U.S. House of Representatives (1989-2011)

"Once again Larry Kryske is back to uncover more about Winston Churchill, one of the most effective and inspirational leaders of all time. Larry's knowledge and experience as a leader make him unusually qualified to relate Churchill's wisdom to 21st century leaders."

Dr. James E. Auer, Director, Auer U.S. – Japan Center, Professor Emeritus, Vanderbilt University

"Churchill Without Blood, Sweat, or Tears
takes the mystery out of leadership and
what makes a great leader. Well done!"

Captain H. Wyman Howard, Jr., U.S. Navy (Ret.)

"No one understands Churchill and his leadership like Larry Kryske! *Churchill Without Blood, Sweat, or Tears* eloquently captures and clearly articulates the basic tenets and simple truths of Churchill and how you can apply them as a successful leader!"

Rear Admiral Scott Hebner, U.S. Navy (Ret.)

"Churchill Without Blood, Sweat, or Tears is easy to read and makes its points quickly and painlessly. The 'Action This Day' questions at the end of each chapter are a wonderful device."

Richard H. Knight, Jr.
Attorney at Law, Nashville, Tennessee

"A quick read! The leadership concepts are understandable and readily applicable. This book delivers more than it promises!"

John Henry King
Economic Development Director
City of Bowie, Maryland

"A practical work painstakingly researched and presented. Churchill's leadership has never been more needed than today."

Thomas F. Gede
Attorney at Law, San Francisco, California

Ready, BEGIN!
Practical Strategies for Cultivating Courage

"Leadership expert and Churchill scholar Larry Kryske has done it again with a book on courage that will become the standard rule book. *Ready, BEGIN!* is a wonderful gift to a university setting and the business world."

Dr. Steve Gruber
Former Adjunct Prof. of Philosophy & Ethics,
Cambridge College

"This readable book challenges us to commit to acts that change and strengthen our businesses and communities."

Dr. Hylan B. Lyon, Jr.
Former member, President's Science Advisors Office

"Courage is the key element in business success! Larry Kryske hits the target with a broad array of useful principles that will help business leaders become more effective."

Daniel C. Libera
President and Founder, Eagle Crest, Inc.

"The only leadership book that discusses how to be courageous!"

Ben Boerner
Former President, Texas Grain & Feed Association

The Churchill Factors: Creating Your Finest Hour

"Awesome book! Winston Churchill overcame overwhelming obstacles to become a great leader. *The Churchill Factors* can help anyone unlock the secrets of creating his or her finest hour."

Duvall Y. Hecht
Founder, President, and CEO, Books on Tape, Inc.

"*The Churchill Factors* is an important tool for current and future leaders wanting to apply the wisdom of the greatest leader of the twentieth century."

Richard Langworth, CBE
Founder, International Churchill Society
Editor, *Churchill by Himself*

"People from all walks of life, including industry, education, business, nonprofit, professional, and government, can benefit from reading and adopting the precepts of this extraordinary book. There is a gold mine of nuggets to be unearthed by the reader."

J. W. Brasher
Vice President (retired), Ingalls Shipbuilding, Inc.

"The goal-setting chapters were the best I have found on the subject. I also liked the author's encouragement concerning taking risks and overcoming obstacles."

John-Edward Alley
Attorney at Law, Tampa, Florida

CHURCHILL
WITHOUT BLOOD, SWEAT, OR TEARS

CHURCHILL

WITHOUT BLOOD, SWEAT, OR TEARS

Lawrence M. Kryske
Commander, United States Navy (Ret.)

HOMEPORT PUBLISHING

Front cover illustration: Rahul Nandram

Back Cover: *His Finest Hour* by L. M. Kryske, oil on canvas,
9" x 12", 30 November 1987

Cover design: Joni McPherson

Library of Congress Control Number: 2017915418

ISBN: 978-0-692-94017-4

**HOMEPORT
PUBLISHING**

www.YourFinestHour.com

Dedicated to:

**My beloved Naomi
and the magical times we have
enjoyed in Hampstead, London**

CONTENTS

DETERMINATION

VICTORY

PREFACE

A jaunty V for victory, defiant speeches, and an ever-present cigar—these are the trademarks by which most people recognize Winston Churchill. Still others see a towering leader and a life full of extraordinary achievements. Both views are valid.

Sir Winston Leonard Spencer Churchill was a twentieth-century Renaissance man—a statesman and warrior, an administrator and historian, an orator and journalist, a landscape oil painter and novelist, and even a bricklayer.

Few realize that Churchill's road to greatness was neither straight nor smooth. He had to wage a constant battle with defeats, doubts, despair, and depression. By employing three critical factors, he turned adversity into advantage. With them he achieved impressive accomplishments. And by using them, he forged a productive and successful life.

These singular factors—vision, courage, and determination—I call the "Churchill factors." In 2000, I first described these elements in a leadership book, *The Churchill Factors: Creating Your Finest Hour*.

Churchill Without Blood, Sweat or Tears will reintroduce you to these factors but in more detail. This short book can be considered an executive overview for the leader who wants to know the "what" and "how" about Churchill's leadership success. The goal is to provide a simple, fast, complete, and understandable roadmap without getting bogged down in a biographic assessment of the Churchill story (his early life, his wilderness years, his finest hour, etc.).

I have spent all my adult life largely pursuing two endeavors. First, I discovered Winston Churchill on the day he died in 1965. His life and leadership have been an unending source of curiosity, study, application, and enjoyment.

Second, I have been involved in leadership since high school. I served as a career naval officer. I participated on teams (often leading them) of private school administrators, teachers, and nonprofit boards. Finally, as a professional speaker, seminar leader, and facilitator, I guided over a hundred thousand individuals to achieve higher levels of leadership, teamwork, and innovation.

Winston Churchill painted his life on a grand canvas. The colors on his gifted palette included: exuberance and resolution, optimism and boldness, congeniality and tenacity, and decisiveness and flexibility, as well as resilience and magnanimity.

The main objective of this book is to present "applied Churchill." Practical, timely insights about Churchill's leadership strategies will enable the reader to use them without delay! These best practices for leadership helped Churchill lead his nation to victory and can likewise guide you to success.

Lawrence M. Kryske
30 November 2017
Plano, Texas

INTRODUCTION

by

Rear Admiral Curtis A. Kemp, U.S. Navy (Ret.)

When you think of Sir Winston Churchill, how can you not think about impactful leadership?

By way of background, the author and I served together as junior officers in the Navy on our first assignments in the guided missile destroyer, *USS Parsons (DDG 33),* homeported in Yokosuka, Japan. We were both shipmates and roommates and part of a "band of brothers" who served under three different commanding officers during our time onboard. Each of these leaders possessed different personalities, and each completed successful careers in the Navy. Thus began our leadership lessons in our military careers. Even then, the author was an avid student and ardent admirer of Winston Churchill.

Over the years during three separate careers, I've had the privilege to work *for* excellent leaders, work *alongside* excellent leaders, and work *with* excellent leaders who were responsible to me. I have come to believe that at its most basic level, leadership is about "influence" and "getting necessary things done."

I've also learned that a good leader thinks constructively and continually embraces a strong sense of hope, as well as always inspiring hope throughout the team, whether that is two people or a nation, as in Winston Churchill's case. Additionally, a leader creates momentum, thereby overcoming inertia and accelerating movement towards the vision.

I've discovered along my journey that mistakes are just as valuable as successes in our leadership education. Although most of us probably think of Churchill during his time as Prime Minister of Great Britain, he held many leadership roles prior to this time and experienced some significant failures and disappointments. The author will show clearly how Churchill learned from these times of pruning such that by the time that Churchill was Prime Minister during World War II, he was exactly the right leader, in the right job, at the right time, in a most demanding season. Some would say that he was groomed "for such a time as this."

Psychologist Dr. Angela Lee Duckworth conducts studies on those who succeed in the face of adversity compared to those who fall short. She determined that those who achieved higher probabilities of overcoming demanding environments possessed more "grit," which she defines as "passion plus perseverance." When we think about those two characteristics both individually and in tandem, we most certainly can see that Winston Churchill was a man of grit. He exuded passion in his approach to all endeavors, and his dogged sense of determination was clearly evident in his demanding expectations first of himself and then of others.

Don't you wish that you could have been a fly on the wall observing Winston Churchill throughout his days during World War II to see how he focused his time, how he interacted with others, and how and why he did things the way he did? With this book in hand, and due to the author's decades of extensive research on Winston Churchill, you are going to get that virtual opportunity of keen insights filled with valuable leadership lessons. These will not be theoretical classroom leadership lessons but rather solid practical tips that you can put to use immediately.

After over twenty-five years in the Navy, I attended a senior leadership conference at which the Chief of Naval Operations (CNO) challenged each of us that as part of our continuing leadership development, we should be reading a book on leadership every month. I thought: "He's got to be kidding. I've been learning leadership lessons in every job I've held in the Navy." But since I admired and respected the CNO, I started a more regular reading program of books on leadership topics. I never quite met his "book a month" challenge, but what I did learn is that we should never stop studying and learning from others.

In my current organization, we have a saying that: "Priorities are what we do. Everything else is just talk." As you read this book, stand by to start making changes in your leadership habits, including clearly laying out your critical priorities for each day. Don't let anything interfere with making diligent progress along your leadership journey of development. And if any barriers are thrown before you, remember: "*Never give in. Never give in. Never, never, never, never …*"

Admiral Kemp is the C12 Group
Managing Chair, Northern Virginia.

1

THE CHURCHILL FACTORS

Throughout his long military and political life, Winston Churchill employed a simple but workable strategy to overcome adversity and achieve victory.

First, he identified an outcome that he wished to achieve. Second, overcoming fear, he boldly took those first few critical steps. Third, despite all obstacles, he persevered until he achieved the result he sought.

In other words, he first established a compelling vision. Next, he got into action with courage. Finally, he followed through with determination until he achieved his vision. Vision, courage, and determination are the three key factors which can collectively be called the "Churchill factors."

Here are some instances when Winston Churchill used this vision, courage, and determination approach:

- **When he wrote a book.** Churchill authored forty-three book-length works in seventy-two volumes (more than twelve million words) including autobiographies, memoirs, histories, biographies, collections of speeches and newspaper articles, and two works of fiction (a novel, *Savrola*, published in 1900, and a short story, *The Dream*, written in 1947 and published posthumously in 1966). He conceived a compelling topic, boldly put himself at risk before his readers, and kept writing and rewriting until he completed his story.

- **When he gave a speech.** Churchill made approximately three thousand speeches (more than five million words). Many of them ring with an audacity and eloquence rarely found. As Edward R. Murrow, and later President Kennedy, observed, "He mobilized the English language and sent it into battle." A speech often entailed as many as twenty hours of practice before he delivered it to his audience.

- **When he cultivated an alliance with President Franklin Roosevelt and America.** Churchill and FDR exchanged letters, cables, telegrams, notes, and telephone calls (Churchill sent 945 and Roosevelt sent 743) and met face to face for a combined 113 days during World War II.

- **When he helped modernize the Royal Navy.** As First Lord of the Admiralty prior to the First World War, Churchill improved professional education for naval officers to create captains of war from captains of ships. He promoted, among hundreds of enhancements, the conversion of the Royal Navy from coal to oil and the development of an air arm for the Royal Navy.

- **When he warned his nation about the menacing rise of Nazism.** During his years in the political wilderness, he recognized the threat posed by Adolf Hitler and the burgeoning military establishment in Germany. Churchill perceived quickly the true nature of Hitler as evil personified. In speeches, newspaper articles, and books, he was a lone voice sounding the alarm.

- **When he alerted the world to the territorial ambitions of the Soviet Union.** Churchill adopted the phrase the "iron curtain" of Soviet domination in Europe in a speech at Westminster College in Fulton, Missouri, in 1946. He sensed the real motivations of the Soviets even after they were an ally in war. With persistence, he gave impassioned speeches to warn of the dangers to world peace.

- **When he assumed administrative responsibilities in Cabinet level positions.** Churchill served in eleven cabinet posts (actually twelve if his position as Minister of Defense while he was Prime Minister in World War II is counted), including both First Lord of the Admiralty and Prime Minister twice. Churchill's prodigious administrative output is thoroughly documented in memoranda, notes, letters, and instructions that exceed two million words.

- **When he painted.** Churchill created almost five hundred and fifty oil paintings, primarily impressionist landscape scenes. He approached his canvas the way a military commander would approach a battlefield. With bold, thickly painted colors, he divided and conquered his foe.

Churchill was the first son of Lord Randolph Churchill, a prominent and magnetic British politician, and Jennie Jerome, a beautiful American socialite. He was born in 1874. Churchill was the product of this English-speaking union of an Englishman and an American, a geopolitical theme he was to promote during both his terms as prime minister.

Churchill's life has been thoroughly documented. Aside from his own works, there are approximately two thousand biographies, histories, and memoirs involving him directly and indirectly. Few leaders are more recognizable in photographs. It is estimated that over 30,000 photos have been taken of Churchill. He has been the subject of numerous novels and motion pictures. In 2017 alone, three movies, *Churchill*, *Dunkirk*, and *The Darkest Hour*, related to Churchill.

> *"We shall go on to the end . . . We shall fight on the beaches, we shall fight on the landing grounds, we shall fight in the fields and in the streets . . . We shall never surrender."*
> **Winston S. Churchill**

Before you assume that Churchill led a comfortable, aristocratic life, remember that he suffered from poor health, had a lisp, had an unloving father and a distant mother (until he was an adult), endured the curse of depression, lost a child, and experienced many personal setbacks, including being removed from high political office twice.

Despite the adversities he encountered, his achievements, productivity, resilience, and reputation as a leader continue to inspire new generations. Vision, courage, and determination worked for Winston Churchill. They gave him victory. Most important, they will work for you, too.

2

CHURCHILL'S STRATEGY FOR SUCCESS

Summarizing Churchill's approach to both life and leadership involves three elements:

VISION + COURAGE + DETERMINATION

Churchill realized that each of these individual steps was simple. Each was simple, but not easy! That is, it was simple to understand, but it was not easy to achieve.

Vision was the first and by far the simplest step. Most people, Churchill included, have some experience developing a compelling vision.

Courage was the most difficult step. Mental and perhaps physical inertia can prevent an individual from moving forward. Churchill asserted that taking those first few steps involved moral and physical courage. Pursuing a vision entailed taking risk, enduring ridicule, and possibly experiencing failure.

Determination was the longest step. The attainment of one's vision requires discipline and dedication to prevail across the most difficult obstacles until the vision has been achieved. Churchill doggedly pursued his desired result. A sustained commitment over a finite time frame characterizes the final step in the methodology.

Vision, courage, and determination are not effective independent of each other. The three *synergize*, that is, work together to create new possibilities:

- Vision without courage and determination leads to hopelessness—you see it, but you do not believe you can achieve it!

- Courage without vision and determination leads to tilting at windmills, taking on too many tasks, and creating challenges that lead nowhere.

- Finally, determination without vision or courage makes us rigid, dogmatic, and more likely to place the blame for our lack of progress on others.

Churchill's skillful use of the three elements yielded the successful achievement he called victory.

Vision, courage, and determination, however, possess several subtleties and nuances that demand a better understanding if we are to apply them as Churchill did. The process takes the three Churchill factors and expands their domains, first into a medium- and then into a fine-grain examination.

> *"We must be united, we must be undaunted, we must be inflexible. Our qualities and deeds must burn and glow through the gloom . . . until they become the veritable beacon of . . . salvation."*
> **Winston S. Churchill**

Churchill's behavior revealed that the highway to vision was made up of three merging lanes: discernment, passion, and innovation. Churchill possessed significant strengths in each of these three areas. They enabled him to plant the seeds of improvements in the Royal Navy, the Ministry of Munitions, and most important, in his wartime leadership as Prime Minister and Minister of Defense.

Churchill's courage entailed two elements: clarity of purpose and taking action. Whether he was escaping from a prisoner-of-war camp during the Boer War or voicing an unpopular point of view during the Cold War, Churchill displayed both physical and moral courage.

Finally, his determination was characterized by two essentials: motivation and resilience. Once he took a stand, Churchill proved to be tenacious, perseverant, and irrepressible as he pursued his visions. He consistently bounced back from setbacks and barriers that impeded his way forward.

By adroitly using vision, courage, and determination, Churchill grew into a heroic leader, a brilliant strategist, and a respected statesman who achieved incredible victories.

Therefore, Churchill's example gives us a simple equation for victory and success:

VISION
+
COURAGE
+
DETERMINATION
=
VICTORY

VISION

3

VISION

Winston Churchill was a man of vision, foresight, prophecy, and destiny. He never lacked compelling visions. Whether he wanted to create "landships" (ultimately called tanks) or to capture in oils the fading sunset on the Atlas Mountains, he instinctively sought endeavors worthy of his fertile imagination, his indomitable will, and his unstoppable drive.

For Churchill, a vision could be a result, goal, purpose, objective, or outcome.

> *"You ask, what is our aim? I can answer in one word: Victory—victory at all costs, victory in spite of all terror, victory, however long and hard the road may be; for without victory, there is no survival."*
> **Winston S. Churchill**

Some of Churchill's visions could be expressed simply, yet others might be abundantly detailed. He knew what he wanted to achieve, and he employed whatever resources necessary for their accomplishment.

Fortunately, Churchill was a believer in the written word. His thoughts, observations, and insights were set down in words thereby allowing future generations to see how his mind operated. His monumental war memoirs, his six-volume *The World Crisis* (about World War I) and his six-volume *Second World War*, reveal he often was involved in extremely detailed discussions involving technological, operational, and geopolitical subjects.

Frequently his visions involved an outcome critical to national survival, such as countering a possible Nazi invasion. In this case, the time domain for the desired result might be in months. On the other hand, his goal of becoming a polished parliamentary speaker entailed years of preparation.

Churchill avoided looking too far ahead, knowing that he had to focus on the most urgent and important problems first. Nevertheless, he devoted some of his mental energies to possible actions in the future that were logical consequences of current activities.

> *"We shape our buildings, and*
> *afterwards our buildings shape us."*
> **Winston S. Churchill**

Each vision, however, created in him a sense of excitement, because the more daunting and compelling the challenge, the more engaged he became. Furthermore, since Churchill often had to persuade the War Cabinet or Parliament of his proposals, he needed more than sufficient evidence to support his visions.

Churchill orchestrated his vision with discernment, passion, and innovation.

****

Winston Churchill recognized the importance of taking action. During the Second World War, he placed small red labels with the words "Action This Day" on the instructions and decision papers he sent to his staff. This helped create a sense of urgency that what the staff was doing was vitally important to the war effort.

We, too, must have a sense of urgency. Each day we must take some specific, measurable, time-dependent, compelling actions to achieve our goals.

ACTION THIS DAY

♦ What are the greatest challenges in your life? (Career advancement, professional development, financial independence, etc.)

♦ What are you committed to accomplishing over the next 2-5 years? Why?

♦ What is preventing you from achieving your goals?

♦ By adding one new skill, you might make your goal more achievable. What is that skill?

4

QUALITIES THAT ADVANCE A VISION— DISCERNMENT

Discernment means distinguishing or observing differences or distinctions. An oil painter can discern colors. A musician can discern sounds. People who are proficient at discernment can uncover perceptions from people, places, or things that the average person would not sense.

People pursuing a vision must develop their power of discernment. One way to do this is to seek the highest-quality information available. The most basic form of information is knowledge. Russell Kelfer astutely observed, "When knowledge becomes personal, we get understanding. When we apply understanding, we get wisdom." So, as we pursue our vision, our goal is not just to gather knowledge but to seek understanding and wisdom. That takes discernment!

Although he tended to be more intuitive than logical, Churchill was a master of discernment. Throughout his life, people remarked on his ability to look at a situation or event and derive significant insights that had escaped others who observed the same conditions.

Churchill employed discernment by:

- **Using his maturity to see the world in terms of its boundaries, tendencies, paradoxes, trends, discontinuities, interrelationships.**

- **Looking for the simple solutions embedded in the complex ones.**

- **Considering counter-intuitive solutions.**

- **Being curious to uncover the salient factors inherent in a problem.**

- **Making distinctions**, not simply gathering more information. Distinctions reflect a natural interplay or interrelationship among information. Examples include separating fact from opinion, questions of taste versus questions of judgment, and feeling versus thinking.

- **Establishing whether a problem was special** (having a unique source) **or common** (having a natural source).

Churchill practiced discernment in four distinct areas: priorities and focus, big picture and details, historical perspective, and simplicity.

ACTION THIS DAY

♦ What qualities do you use to control the outcomes in your life that have brought you success? (Being decisive, taking risks, taking charge.)

♦ Has there been any cost to you using these qualities? If so, what are some alternatives to getting results without sacrificing what or who is important to you?

DISCERNMENT 1—PRIORITIES & FOCUS

A compelling vision comes down to priorities. Priorities are derived from the kernel of who we are. What is important to us? What values do we admire? What do we hope to be, do, or have? How much ridicule, pain, and torment are we willing to tolerate to accomplish our vision? Is the issue one of right versus wrong?

Our priority anchors our vision in time and space. It is a starting point. As we commence the vision, courage, and determination process, we might refine our vision. We will get smarter as we learn more about the demands and challenges of achieving our vision. As we learn more, we may choose to be even more specific about the outcome we desire. One way to accelerate this is to focus.

Focus means knowing precisely what is important to accomplish. One behaves more like a laser beam than a searchlight, identifying the single object one wishes to illuminate.

Do not confuse focus with concentration. Focus is a filter through which we see the world. When victory over the Nazis became Churchill's focus, he viewed all necessary activities through this filter. Concentration is restricting one's attention to some specific task. We can give something our undivided attention or we can give our divided attention (multitasking) if our mental capacities are not overtaxed.

Churchill was disciplined and able to cut through overwhelming data and distractions to select the critical target. The things that mattered most received his keenest attention. He was one of those individuals who could juggle dozens of balls without dropping any. He could compartmentalize his brain, keeping critical tasks separated until they needed to be addressed.

His leadership as prime minister during the Second World War was reinforced by his extensive twenty-two years of experience leading and managing the eight different Cabinet positions that he earlier occupied.

> *"Safety first is the road to ruin in war, even if you had the safety, which you have not."*
> **Winston S. Churchill**

As a strategist, Churchill was adept at considering military, political, diplomatic, and economic implications. He favored surprise and intensity (his version of shock and awe) in his military solutions as well as Carl von Clausewitz's dictum of defeating the enemy forces instead of taking territory.

Churchill was a driven man. Whether hoping to please his father, earn medals in war in India, the Sudan, or South Africa, or perform bravely in the trenches of France, he pursued his destiny aggressively and with single-minded passion. His drive created his focus which in turn established his priorities. Churchill focused because he was driven to achieve certain outcomes.

After America joined the Second World War, Churchill looked at all strategic choices through two filters. First, would the efforts that were proposed lead to a shortening of the war? And second, would the efforts prevent the Soviets from amassing more territory and thereby upsetting the strategic balance in the subsequent peace?

By 1943, Churchill recognized that the Allied leaders were the "trustees for the peace of the world." Their actions would influence the circumstances that followed. They needed to avert the kind of calamity that had emerged from the ashes of the First World War (namely, the Second World War).

Churchill could not dismiss Marshal Joseph Stalin's postwar intentions. He was not naïve like Roosevelt, who thought he could win over the Soviet leader with his charm. Churchill observed in 1939 that Russia "is a riddle wrapped in a mystery inside an enigma: but perhaps there is a key. The key is Russian national interest."

World peace following the devastating war would be a chimera unless the Big Three could reach a genuine agreement. At the Tehran Conference in 1943 Churchill noted, "There I sat with the great Russian bear on one side of me, with paws outstretched, and on the other side the great American buffalo, and between the two sat the poor little English donkey who was the only one, the only one of the three, who knew the right way home."

ACTION THIS DAY

♦ **What can you discern better than others?**

♦ **What's your top priority right now?**

DISCERNMENT 2—BIG PICTURE & DETAILS

Think of the big picture as an umbrella that encompasses the "what" rather than the "how." A robust transportation system is a big picture outcome. Fuel-efficient cars and airplanes, safe modern highways and airports, urban subways, and light rail systems are subcomponents.

The big picture can also be equated to the strategy. It is the overarching plan that tends to encompass a longer time domain and does not change easily or often. On the other hand, tactics are more short term and flexible in nature and change as necessary. Many tactics are employed to achieve a strategy.

> *"It is a good thing to stand away*
> *from the canvas from time to time*
> *and take a full view of the picture."*
> **Winston S. Churchill**

In World War II, Churchill embraced an initial strategy of winning the war in three critical geographic locations: the British homeland (the Battle of Britain), the Mediterranean, and the North Atlantic (the Battle of the Atlantic). This approach was supported by tactical benefits conferred by employing radar, ensuring Royal Air Force air superiority over Britain, protecting the Suez Canal (the gateway to the Empire), and utilizing convoys.

Strategically, Churchill was a pragmatist. He evaluated his options differently than other Allied leaders. He favored utilizing opportunities and improvising on them to accommodate rapidly changing situations on the battlefield. This line of thought was more frequently used in tactical applications.

The big picture gives us the overall objective. Details, however, are needed to flesh out the specific actions we will employ to achieve our vision. We need to uncover both the "whys" and "hows." Churchill's prodigious memory allowed him to retain vast amounts of details garnered over a lifetime in leadership and administration.

Detail-oriented people, like Churchill, also ask powerful, probing questions. They look for patterns, trends, and what is missing. They seek to gain insights from data because they want to understand. They will take the time to study the complications they seek to solve.

"You must look at the facts,
because they look at you."
Winston S. Churchill

Churchill's past Cabinet-level experiences gave him a thorough knowledge of the government and all its departments. He was well versed in being able to respond to unforeseen events by tapping the right department to solve the problem.

Churchill's uncanny understanding of both the big picture and the details gave him the ability to use his government effectively during the strains of war. He mobilized a knowledge of operational issues, technological innovations, and governmental and civilian working populations into an effective fighting force.

ACTION THIS DAY

♦ Are you better at the big picture or details?

♦ How can you enhance your ability with the lesser one?

♦ Who can help you with the lesser one? What's stopping you?

DISCERNMENT 3—HISTORICAL PERSPECTIVE

Historical perspective is an awareness of the bigger picture and larger context as related to events in the past. For Churchill, his broad historical judgment enabled him to anticipate and resolve challenges that threatened the fulfillment of his vision.

In general terms his perspective helped him to read the geopolitical tea leaves. He gained a wide-ranging panorama of the past by having extensive experiences and by traveling in time and space via reading.

> *"The longer you look back, the*
> *farther you can look forward."*
> **Winston S. Churchill**

All his adult life Churchill cultivated his viewpoint by thinking about the age-old question of whether "man made the times or times made the man." He believed that great men influenced history.

Churchill did not receive a university education and was largely self-educated. He once reflected, "I am always ready to learn, although I do not always like being taught." He also read prodigiously and had extraordinary recall. He was guided by his maxim, "Persevere towards those objectives which are lighted for us by all the wisdom and inspiration of the past."

Churchill's many histories and biographies helped him to interpret history and its leaders through calibrated eyes. He observed, "A nation that forgets its past has no future."

Churchill used what he learned about the past to give him insights about what might occur in the future. He, however, lived in the present but always had an eye on what lay ahead.

His agile, intuitive mind helped him to connect the dots. Hence, he accurately predicted the coming of World War I, World War II, and the Cold War. He also anticipated the geopolitical moves of Hitler and Stalin.

> *"Study history, study history. In history lie all the secrets of statecraft."*
> **Winston S. Churchill**

Why do we need a broad perspective, historical or experience based? Because it can help us in maneuvering across a hostile landscape of obstacles as we pursue our vision. Churchill comprehended, "We cannot undo the past, but we are bound to pass it in review in order to draw from it such lessons as may be applicable to the future."

ACTION THIS DAY

♦ Does your historical perspective come from reading or experience?

♦ What can you do to get additional perspective?

DISCERNMENT 4—SIMPLICITY

Simplicity is essential in creating a vision. If something is simple, it can be remembered. If it can be remembered, it can be applied. And if it can be applied, then people can benefit from the attainment of the outcomes.

Churchill believed, "Life, which is so complicated and difficult in great matters, nearly always presents itself in simple terms." Keeping things simple keeps them real and authentic.

> *"All the great things are simple and many can be expressed in a single word: freedom; justice; honor; duty; mercy; hope."*
> **Winston S. Churchill**

Churchill could not have earned the trust, respect, and support of the British people during the London Blitz if he were esoteric, pedantic, or complex. Both his actions and his words were simple to understand.

In the scheme of things, crafting simple policies and procedures is often intellectually more difficult. The benefits of simple guidelines lie in the ease of their execution.

Occam's Razor further asserts that for two explanations involving virtually anything, the simpler one is usually better. This is also consistent with laws of nature in which a physical system will always seek the lowest energy state. Churchill felt that one need not expend more effort than is required to get the job done. Churchill correctly observed, "Out of intense complexities, intense simplicities emerge."

ACTION THIS DAY

♦ What complex area in your life or work needs to be simplified?

♦ Is it difficult to decide which of two approaches should be followed?

♦ How can simplicity enhance the way you lead others?

5

QUALITIES THAT ADVANCE A VISION—PASSION

Without passion, a vision will go nowhere. With it, a person is limited only by his or her imagination and will.

Passion is characterized by an intense driving conviction to accomplish an outcome. It is the fuel that propels us to achieve what was previously unachievable.

How did Churchill manifest his zeal? He possessed a furious fire in the belly! He radiated an infectious confident smile on his face, and his eyes blazed with a joyous twinkle! He possessed an unstoppable urge to press forward!

Churchill had a lust for life, challenges and all. He had fun at what he did. It was not the entertainment-park aspect of fun but rather the satisfaction of doing something professionally and personally rewarding. His sense of humor gave him a fuller, more balanced perspective on life.

> *"Soberness and restraint do not necessarily prevent the joyous expression of the human heart."*
> *Winston S. Churchill*

Churchill exhibited passion in four ways: enthusiasm/exuberance, optimism, alliances, and clear communications.

ACTION THIS DAY

♦ What things (e.g. vision, mission, purpose, people, challenges) cause you to be truly passionate?

♦ If you could be or do anything and know you wouldn't fail, what would you be or do?

PASSION 1—ENTHUSIASM/EXUBERANCE

Enthusiasm, the strong excitement of feelings, may be regarded as a barometer of one's passion. Churchill was jubilantly passionate about what he did. But Churchill's contagious enthusiasm rose to even higher levels of elation that must be characterized as exuberance. Exuberance is enthusiasm on steroids!

Churchill called himself, "A man of push and go." What was the source of Churchill's positive energy? Each of us possesses a genius in some area where we perform at a high level. When we operate there, we can be exuberant. We feel creative, joyous, and energized. Churchill had a genius for getting things done, especially outcomes others thought were not possible.

Churchill's buoyant and animated demeanor helped him to promote his ideas. He shaped a positive momentum for plans he originated.

Churchill demonstrated enthusiasm by:

- **Acting with zeal, fervor, and passion.**

- **Resonating the joy** of his own life.

- **Being upbeat and exuding a high energy level.**

- **Thinking positively**.

- **Surrounding himself with positive people.** He enjoyed being with insightful, original thinkers.

- **Doing what he enjoyed doing**.

- **Expressing his sense of humor, wit, and good cheer.**

- **Seeing opportunities** in challenges.

- **Being interested and curious as well as asking probing questions.**

- **Trusting his ability to respond** to trials and tribulations with confidence.

- **Praising heroes** for their sacrifices and successes.

- **Letting his face, voice, gestures, and words reflect animation, excitement, and wonder.**

Churchill possessed ceaseless energy! He was a perpetual-motion machine, a dynamo of drive, force, and power.

Churchill's enthusiasm attracted countless followers. He earned genuine respect from his personal staff as well as military and political colleagues. Even though Churchill was a demanding taskmaster, subordinates possessed an affection and love for their prime minister.

ACTION THIS DAY

♦ What are you most enthusiastic about? How can others tell?

♦ What things make you exuberant? Are you self-conscious about being exuberant?

♦ In what areas could you be more enthusiastic?

PASSION 2—OPTIMISM

Optimists find confidence and hope in the future and see a silver lining in every black cloud. Optimism is a choice, not a delusion, and is born of a belief that one's actions can influence some facet of what's happening. Leaders have a responsibility to be positive if they are to lead effectively. John W. Gardner observed, "A prime function of a leader is to keep hope alive."

Throughout a life burdened with adversity, Churchill recognized the benefits of being upbeat. While he was serving as a battalion commander in the trenches on the Western Front during World War I, he opined that optimism, no matter how difficult, was essential on the battlefield.

> *"What is the use of living, if it be not to strive for noble causes and to make this muddled world a better place for those who live in it after we are gone?"*
> **Winston S. Churchill**

Long hazardous flights from London to North Africa and Russia during the Second World War in a noisy, cold bomber bay did not stifle Churchill's exuberant spirit. A cynical word never escaped his lips despite physical discomforts that distressed his younger traveling companions.

Optimism is a force multiplier. Force multipliers amplify an effort to yield more results. A lever is a force multiplier. You can use it to lift a heavy weight that would have been impossible with unaided human strength.

Churchill was optimistic by:

- **Realistically choosing to see positive possibilities** in the direst of circumstances or challenges.

- **Controlling his emotions.**

- **Being hopeful and keeping hope alive for others.**

- **Smiling at adversity.** Churchill was ready to "take the rough with the smooth."

- **Focusing on what went right** while making corrections to what didn't go well.

- **Realizing that everything has a season. Nothing lasts forever.**

- **Giving himself and others positive and encouraging feedback.**

- **Being solution oriented**.

- **Refraining from blaming others** or circumstances.

- **Anticipating the unthinkable.**

- **Keeping his vision on target.**

During the bleakest hours of the London Blitz, Churchill projected optimism and hope to his beleaguered countrymen. While London was under aerial attack, Churchill ended a speech to the nation with Arthur

Hugh Clough's hopeful words, "But westward, look, the land is bright."

> *"By our courage, our endurance, and our brains, we have made our way in the world to the lasting benefit of mankind. Let us not lose heart. Our future is one of high hope."*
> **Winston S. Churchill**

During the Second World War, Churchill confidently focused on goals and positive expectations and wanted others to do the same. Generals, admirals, and politicians who were defeatists found themselves banished from the ranks of policy makers.

Churchill saw the world as it was and also as it could be. His optimism motivated millions of people who looked with fear at a world of despair. Churchill was never one to sugarcoat the truth. He warned, "Nourish your hopes, but do not overlook realities."

ACTION THIS DAY

◆ On a scale of 1-10 (10 being the highest), how optimistic are you?

◆ Where on the optimism scale do you need to be in order to become a better leader?

◆ What things will you do to see the world, your challenges, and your circumstances more optimistically?

PASSION 3—ALLIANCES

Self-reliance can derail the most inspired vision. Churchill as prime minister, therefore, surrounded himself with people with whom he could collaborate in obtaining needed information and in developing strategies and policies.

> *"Come then, let us go forward*
> *together with our united strength."*
> **Winston S. Churchill**

The way Churchill enrolled others to support his cause involved a deliberate, three-pronged approach. The first involved creating a relationship based on trust. Then he proposed exploring possibilities. This entailed mobilizing arguments, evidence, and context for exploiting mutually beneficial opportunities. Finally, he proposed actions, cementing the commitment with enthusiasm and passion.

Churchill collaborated with his colleagues and listened to their objections, criticisms, and suggestions. He frequently changed his mind when new facts necessitated a change in strategy. Churchill delegated authority to other people. At the same time, he retained responsibility for the final successes or failures of the action.

Churchill effected alliances within his own staff, among his Cabinet ministers and military leaders, and on a higher plane with Roosevelt and Stalin. It was his "Grand Alliance" that transformed the initial wartime losses against the Nazi and Japanese forces into a series of dramatic successes that ultimately achieved victory over tyranny.

Churchill had an alliance with three special advisors who also happened to be his friends: Brendan Bracken (financial and political), Frederick Lindemann (scientific), and Max Beaverbrook (production and the press). Each one helped Churchill navigate areas in which he needed assistance.

Inherent in collaboration was Churchill's need to build his team. He did not have the luxury of going off site and into a calm, safe, encouraging environment to relate with each team member and participate in team building. He had to fight the war with what he had.

Some associates were challenging. For Churchill, the glass was half full. For Field Marshall Alan Brooke, Chief of the Imperial General Staff, the glass was half empty. Together they complemented each other and wove an executable strategy to defeat Hitler.

Britain had already been at war for eight months when Churchill was given the reins of government in 1940. During the tumultuous period of rapid change, he assembled a national government composed of leaders from the major political parties.

ACTION THIS DAY

♦ Do you have a brain trust, mentors, coaches, or special advisors to help you?

PASSION 4—CLEAR COMMUNICATIONS

All human interaction is sourced in mankind's greatest invention, language. Churchill was a master of both written and spoken English. When the world was teetering on the precipice of a new dark age, his heroic words gave hope, strength, and inspiration to frightened people worldwide.

Churchill concluded that effective messaging involved four elements:

- **Simplicity.**
- **Clarity.**
- **Repetition.**
- **Emotional appeal**.

When these elements were all present, people could understand the communication without ambiguity, confusion, distortion, or distraction.

Churchill chose his words well. His uncanny use of simile and metaphor, unexpected humor, and deliberate mispronunciation delighted his listeners. He adroitly used words to manage both the performance and perceptions of his government.

> *"Short words are best and old words when short are the best yet."*
> **Winston S. Churchill**

Churchill's world-renowned speeches followed a consistent formula. Former presidential speechwriter, James C. Humes in *The Sir Winston Method* revealed these to be:

- **An impactful, attention-getting start.**
- **Only one main subject.**
- **Clear, easily understood language.**
- **Word images.**
- **A powerful, passionate ending.**

Two additional components that enhanced Churchill's speeches were his use of theatrics (gestures, pauses, and seemingly spontaneous although preplanned witticisms) and fact-based content.

In an unpublished article in 1897 entitled, "The Scaffolding of Rhetoric," Churchill suggested that an effective speech contained four stylistic elements:

- **A correctness of diction.**
- **Rhythm.**
- **The accumulation of argument.**
- **The use of analogy.**

> *"If you have an important point to make, don't try to be subtle or clever. Use a pile driver. Hit the point once. Then come back and hit it again. Then hit it a third time."*
> **Winston S. Churchill**

Churchill not only spoke clearly, he spoke truthfully. On numerous occasions during the war, he candidly told his countrymen that despite small victories, "things would get worse before they got better."

Churchill's many books and articles reveal that from his earliest works, he possessed a lordly writing style. Few were as adept as he in using the most precise and appropriate word. Most of Churchill's literary works were dictated, so listening to them gives the best means of capturing the full grandeur of his rhetoric. On a good night, he could dictate five thousand words. Undeniably, Churchill can be considered the greatest dictator of all time!

> *"Writing a book is an adventure. To begin with it is a toy, an amusement. Then it becomes a mistress, and then it becomes a master, and then it becomes a tyrant. And in the last stage, just as you are about to be reconciled to your servitude, you slay the monster and fling him to the public."*
> **Winston S. Churchill**

In addition to his speeches and books were millions of words in letters, white papers, policy statements, directives, orders, and memoranda. Churchill was a firm believer in avoiding verbal orders. He always put orders and instructions on paper to avoid misunderstanding. Therefore, he left a detailed paper trail to accompany his leadership and administration of Cabinet postings.

Nonlinear outcomes during the Second World War meant that Churchill had to be skillful at crisis management. Defeats and losses on the battlefield required both military and verbal containment and damage control. His effective communications restored confidence and gave encouragement, especially in the early years of the war.

ACTION THIS DAY

♦ What challenges do you have making a presentation to a group of people? How well does your message motivate their performance?

♦ Do you avoid verbal orders? Have you experienced misunderstandings in the past by those carrying out your requests?

6

QUALITIES THAT ADVANCE A VISION—
INNOVATION

Innovation, what Dr. Jared Diamond called, "the most human of characteristics," is a key element in the achievement of a vision. It brings into existence new ideas, methods, or devices. Most do not involve truly unique creations such as the phonograph, telephone, or Dr. Pepper. The item, nonetheless, is still regarded as an innovation if it is new to the vision seeker.

Winston Churchill not only harnessed the power of innovation but was himself quite the innovator. Personally, he developed his siren suit, a one-piece jumpsuit he could quickly don as the air raid sirens wailed. He put speeches on paper in psalm form to facilitate their usefulness as a delivery aid.

He stimulated and encouraged development of tanks, the Royal Naval Air Service, artificial harbors for D-Day, and a brilliant (although poorly executed) Dardanelles strategy to outflank the Germans during the First World War. (Had Admiral David "damn-the-torpedoes-full-speed-ahead" Farragut been at the Dardanelles instead of Admiral de Robeck, the course of history might have turned out differently.)

While at the Ministry of Munitions in 1917, Churchill streamlined the massive organization by downsizing and simplifying it. He inherited a department of 50 departments (all reporting to him) managed by 12,000 bureaucrats who oversaw 2.8 million workers in 27,000 firms—a huge unwieldy morass.

Churchill created a Munitions Council of ten individuals, each responsible for five related areas of production, who would report to him directly. He achieved his goal of speeding up decision-making and war armaments production. (The Ministry of Munitions was responsible for army armaments only. The Admiralty was responsible for navy armaments. Churchill, however, controlled steel that was vital to both naval shipbuilding and army needs.)

Churchill wanted his senior leaders to wear two hats. The first was to lead and manage their specific areas of responsibility (the details). Second, he wanted them to come together as a team to think about what was best for the entire ministry concerning war production (the big picture).

In effect, he established an early form of total quality management "process action teams" as well as an "executive steering committee" at a time when the quality guru, Dr. W. Edwards Deming, was just graduating from high school.

"You must put your head into the lion's mouth if performance is to be a success."
Winston S. Churchill

Churchill appreciated the realities about innovation: It is a tool, a means to some end, which like mastery, takes time. Innovators must live with the problem to be solved and let solutions percolate and brew. Failures are necessary because that is how we learn. Innovators seek the truth. The question "what if" is always on their lips. Political and scientific spin will not result in viable innovations.

Innovations often necessitated security (and patience) to protect programs until they could best be employed. The British developed Window (long strips of aluminum foil dropped from a bomber) to deceive German radars and hide the planes. It was not used for a year after its development.

Innovation is the confluence of three rivers: trust, creativity, and courage.

ACTION THIS DAY

♦ Are you more failure adverse or innovation friendly?

♦ Innovation cannot be legislated nor does it follow a schedule. It must be cultivated. Can you live with these conditions?

INNOVATION 1—TRUST

Trust is the assured reliance on the character, strength, and competence of a person. Being worthy and able yield trust. It is built on mutual respect, openness, honesty, and effective communications (clear speaking and intentional listening).

Churchill's upstanding character shone brightly among other national and international contemporaries. Like all people, Churchill had feet of clay, but not when it came to honesty and integrity. He was trustworthy and relished seeking the truth. He offered, "I would sooner be right than consistent," which explains why he shed party loyalty.

> *"This truth is incontrovertible. Panic may resent it, ignorance may deride it, malice may distort it, but there it is."*
> **Winston S. Churchill**

Churchill respected the importance of trust in his dealings with President Roosevelt and his personal representatives Harry Hopkins and Averell Harriman. Later Churchill established trust with Stalin and General Eisenhower. He also built it with his generals, admirals, Bletchley Park cryptographic specialists, and the scientific communities who developed the many innovations (like radar and ASDIC, an early version of sonar) used in the Second World War.

ACTION THIS DAY

♦ How do you evaluate a person to determine if he or she can be trusted? Do you have certain subtle tests?

♦ What do you do to build trust with someone? Which things challenge you most?

♦ Trust and truthfulness go hand in hand. When, if ever, are white lies permissible and possibly necessary?

INNOVATION 2—CREATIVITY

Creativity is the ability to produce something using one's imaginative talents. All innovative efforts are creative, but not all creative efforts are innovative. Innovation is simply applied creativity.

Churchill was a master of generating new, fresh, original, and endless ideas. As prime minister, he kept his personal staff and military leaders awake at night with his incessant bombardment of suggestions of how to do their jobs better. He reframed problems by looking at things in new ways.

> *"The stronger your imagination,*
> *the more variegated your universe."*
> **Winston S. Churchill**

Churchill's agile mind, coupled with his imagination, interest, and fascination in myriads of subjects, served as the fountainhead of his innovative powers. He realized that "imagination without deep and full knowledge is a snare." Whether he was crafting a speech to inspire his countrymen or suggesting a strategy to overcome a particular military deficit, Churchill creatively harnessed his formative powers in his pursuit of winning the war against the Nazis.

The operational deception plans devised to protect the D-Day landing owe their innovative success to Churchill's impetus, cultivation, and support. British cover and deception tactics (e.g., phony armies, communications spoofing, political warfare, dummy aircraft and tanks, double agents, a corpse in uniform with forged papers, and counter espionage) confused the Nazis about the future Allied invasion at Normandy.

> *"In wartime, truth is so precious that she should always be attended by a bodyguard of lies."*
> **Winston S. Churchill**

Churchill's landscape oil paintings give a glimpse of his creativity. He painted thickly and used bright colors that magnified the depths of his personal rainbow. His bold, quick brush strokes reflected his unabashed exuberance. He also painted with supreme confidence both on the canvas with oils and on his universe with his thoughts, words, and deeds.

Churchill used nontraditional problem solving that stemmed from his intuitive approach rather than devising routine, conventional-wisdom solutions. He needed creative ways for countering the overwhelming military juggernaut fielded by the Nazis.

ACTION THIS DAY

♦ **Are you being as creative as possible?**

♦ **What can you do to increase your creativity?**

65

INNOVATION 3—COURAGE

Courage is the critical bridge between knowing what to do and doing it. It fills in the gap, becoming the execution phase of the innovative process. (Courage is also the critical element of the three Churchill factors. A more detailed discussion of courage and how Churchill cultivated it will be found in the next section of this book.)

All three elements of innovation—trust, creativity, and courage—put vision seekers at risk. The actions they take will not guarantee success. Other people may not choose to trust them. Their creative ideas, insights, and approaches may be flawed. And finally, when the propitious moment arrives, they may not possess the necessary courage to act.

Each person has a different risk threshold, and risk engenders fear. Fear may lead to failure, but failure often is the wellhead of innovation.

Churchill comprehended that it took courage to innovate. It took courage to challenge the status quo and pursue a new vision. Churchill heard in both military and political circles all the sacred cows that competed with his ideas:

- We've never done it that way before!
- What we have is good enough as is!
- It will never work!
- We've already tried that!
- It can't be done!

Churchill understood that as children, people were naturally courageous. They took great risks. They learned to walk, ride a bicycle, and climb trees, sometimes even climbing out on a limb. Churchill retained many childlike qualities all his life: wonder, curiosity, exuberance, and fearlessness.

Open-minded people are intellectually honest. Churchill genuinely sought to understand the truth. He feared neither change nor the unknown. He assessed ideas from multiple perspectives and points of view. He engaged the universe by seeking to learn all he could, wherever he could, whenever he could. Churchill not only changed the paradigm of wartime leadership but was one of the first to foresee the realities and needs of the postwar world.

> *"The empires of the future*
> *are the empires of the mind."*
> **Winston S. Churchill**

Yet Churchill gathered that no organization can be innovative in everything that it does. According to his chief military assistant, General Hastings Lionel "Pug" Ismay, Churchill "venerated tradition," especially with respect to the honors and ceremony of the military. He was open minded, however, with new technology and tactics. Thus, Churchill reached a balance between tradition and innovation.

Churchill grasped the importance of getting smart quickly once the war with the Nazis commenced. He assembled his nation's best scientific and technological experts and launched them in finding tractable solutions quickly for their direst needs. The rapid development of radar, cryptography, landing craft, and artificial harbors grew out of Churchill's innovative impetus. The risks were great, but failure to innovate would have been fatal.

ACTION THIS DAY

♦ Which sacred cows do you have to fight in your work? Why are your business associates so invested in these mindsets?

♦ How can you convince them to attempt a new or better approach?

♦ On a scale of 1 to 10 (10 is the highest), rate yourself on your open mindedness. What do you need to change? Why?

COURAGE

7

COURAGE

Courage is what transforms a leader into a legend. Churchill knew that leadership was the art of getting things done with other people and acting with courage to achieve specific, measurable, time-dependent outcomes. Visioning and planning are only part of the leadership equation. Churchill's example revealed that translating visions into reality took courage and determination.

> *"Courage is rightly esteemed the first of human qualities because it is the quality which guarantees all others."*
> **Winston S. Churchill**

Throughout his life, Churchill displayed courage when he:

- **Exposed himself to physical danger.**
- **Took an unpopular political stand.**
- **Refused to compromise his values.**
- **Confronted fear by taking action.**
- **Did something he had never done before.**

People are not courageous for the sake of being courageous. Rather, they are courageous because they feel compelled to pursue their vision. Courage is the critical step in the Churchill factors process but remains only a means to attaining an outcome.

Churchill fought on two different fronts to be courageous: clarity of purpose and taking action.

ACTION THIS DAY

♦ Do you see yourself as a courageous person? Why or why not?

♦ Where is courage needed in your personal and professional life?

♦ How easy is it to do something you've never done before? Is it terrifying? Challenging? Exhilarating?

8

QUALITIES THAT CULTIVATE COURAGE— CLARITY OF PURPOSE

Churchill was introspective, carefully examining his own thoughts and feelings. He was extremely clear about:

- **Who he was.**
- **What he stood for.**
- **What he valued.**
- **What he was prepared to do.**

His clarity of purpose was a house whose foundation was constructed on bedrock, not shifting sands.

> *"We shall not be judged by the criticisms of our opponents but by the consequences of our acts."*
> **Winston S. Churchill**

Courage grows out of clarity of purpose. When his subsequent actions were congruent with his beliefs and values, Churchill could experience a purposeful life without shame.

The greater Churchill's clarity of purpose, the more he could find the inner strength necessary to face alarming situations requiring both physical and moral courage. Dr. Paul L. Escamilla observed that "Crisis often creates clarity." Throughout Churchill's military and political life, he found himself dealing with crises. These events reinforced his beliefs and attitudes about what he held dear and inviolable.

Churchill developed his clarity of purpose in three ways: introspection, values, and benchmarking heroes.

ACTION THIS DAY

♦ Who are you? What do you aspire to be, to do, and to have?

♦ What do you stand for? Why? After you answer "why," ask "why" again for a total of five iterations of "why." Look for the root cause of your stand.

♦ How do you prioritize your life with respect to family, work, nationality, faith?

CLARITY OF PURPOSE 1—INTROSPECTION

As Prime Minister, Churchill demonstrated the need to examine his actions especially in light of the feedback he received from his advisors. This took the form of a daily introspective "examen" in which he conducted a personal inquiry and investigation. He wanted to ensure that he was true to his values, that he could not fault himself for not doing more, and that he was making a positive difference.

> *"Each night before I go to bed, I try myself by Court Martial to see if I have done something really effective during the day."*
> **Winston S. Churchill**

In his early life, Churchill was concerned about taking heroic actions under fire, earning medals for bravery, and not shaming his family name.

Churchill changed his political party affiliation twice in his sixty-two-year Parliamentary career, earning the lifelong enmity of many of his colleagues. He "crossed the floor" in the House of Commons in 1904, changing from the Conservative Party (colloquially called the Tory Party) to the Liberal Party.

> *"The only guide to a man is his conscience, the only shield to his memory is the rectitude and sincerity of his actions."*
> **Winston S. Churchill**

In 1924, he returned to the Conservatives. He changed party both times for following values that were important to him. Churchill politically could be classified as a liberal Tory and believed in Tory Democracy, as did his father, Lord Randolph Churchill.

Churchill's moral compass was additionally reinforced by his faith in a destiny that he believed compelled him to perform valuable services to his country.

ACTION THIS DAY

♦ Do you have a daily period of introspection to evaluate your personal performance? Do you do this in the beginning of the day, sometime during the work day, or in the evening?

♦ How important is it for you to follow your moral compass if the company you work for has unethical, unsafe, or questionable practices?

CLARITY OF PURPOSE 2—VALUES

A value reflects a person's principles or standards of behavior. In other words, it represents a person's judgment of what he or she considers important in life.

What values did Winston Churchill hold? Looking at his words and deeds, one can discern the following. Churchill's quotation follows each one.

Constitutionality—"The central principle of civilization is the subordination of the ruling authority to the settled customs of the people and their will as expressed through the Constitution."

Courage—"We must never lose our faith and our courage, never must we fail in exertion and resolve."

Determination—"Let us do our utmost—all that is in us—for the good of all."

Duty—"Let us therefore brace ourselves to our duties, and so bear ourselves that, if the British Empire and its Commonwealth last for a thousand years, men will still say, 'This was their finest hour.'"

Freedom—"The cause of freedom has in it a recuperative power and virtue which can draw from misfortune new hope and new strength."

Generosity—"Generosity is always wise."

Liberty—"There is no limit to the ingenuity of man if it is properly and vigorously applied under conditions of peace and justice."

Magnanimity—"As we have triumphed, so we may be merciful; as we are strong, so we can afford to be generous."

Optimism—"For myself I am an optimist—it does not seem to be much use being anything else."

Patriotism—"I admire men who stand up for their country."

Responsibility—"The price of greatness is responsibility."

Resolve—"It is wonderful what great strides can be made when there is a resolute purpose behind them."

Victory—"Victory is sure, and it will belong to all who have not faltered or flinched or wearied on the long road."

Another quality Churchill possessed was his public-spirited nature. He was genuinely concerned with the well-being of others. He more than any other contemporary leader during the Second World War personified the indomitable spirit of Englishmen. He sincerely believed, "In politics when you are in doubt what to do, do nothing . . . when you are in doubt what to say, say what you really think."

"I . . . adopted quite early in life a system of believing what I wanted to believe, while at the same time leaving reason to pursue unfettered whatever paths she was capable of treading."
Winston S. Churchill

Churchill's values gave him an internal set of standards by which he led his life. Whether in the military or in politics, he chose to link his personal identity and aspirations with successes that would also benefit his country and its countrymen.

ACTION THIS DAY

♦ Which values do you stand for? Follow the five "why" root cause analysis again with each one.

♦ Prioritize your values from most important to least.

♦ Have you ever had to stand up and be counted because you could not violate your value system?

♦ Have your values given you additional strength to face challenging futures and difficult decisions? If so, when?

79

CLARITY OF PURPOSE 3—
BENCHMARKING HEROES

Nothing gives us a better picture of courageous behavior than the real-life examples of other people. Churchill learned to model heroic behavior by studying the lives of individuals who took courageous and noble actions in the face of adversity.

A person may either be intimidated or inspired by heroes. Clearly, Churchill chose to be inspired by and even emulated many of his.

Several personages served as a role model for him:

Lord Randolph Churchill—His father, who was a colorful, rising politician whom contemporaries thought would one day lead his party and perhaps become prime minister. He was the subject of a two-volume biography by his son. Churchill even adopted his father's political and speaking style, dress, and brash behavior.

John Churchill, the First Duke of Marlborough— Winston Churchill's famous statesman-warrior ancestor, victor of the Battle of Blenheim in 1704, and subject of a four-volume work by Churchill. Churchill admired the Duke's diplomatic dexterity. The Duke served five monarchs during his tenure, as later did his famous descendant, Sir Winston S. Churchill.

Horatius, the Captain of the Gate—Macaulay's *Lays of Ancient Rome* (which Churchill learned as a schoolboy at Harrow) illuminated the daring actions of Horatius and two other Roman soldiers who prevented an invading army from crossing a bridge into Rome and sacking the poorly defended city. Horatius made a tremendous impression on young Churchill.

T. E. Lawrence (of Arabia)—Lawrence served as Churchill's special advisor on Arab affairs when he was Colonial Secretary after the First World War. His heroic, unconventional guerrilla tactics enthralled Churchill. Lawrence once came downstairs at Churchill's country house, Chartwell, resplendently attired in the robes of a prince of Arabia.

Thomas Macaulay and Edward Gibbon—Two English historians, writers, and politicians who made history come alive for Winston Churchill. Churchill emulated elements of their writing styles that gave maturity and later gravitas to his own.

Admiral Lord Horatio Nelson—This most famous Royal Navy admiral defeated the French fleet at Trafalgar in 1805, giving Britain command of the seas and security for over a century. Mention of Nelson's epic death at the end of the battle routinely brought tears to Churchill's eyes.

Napoleon Bonaparte—Churchill admired Napoleon's military and political acumen. He wanted to write a biography of Napoleon but never did.

William Pitt (the Younger)—Pitt at age twenty-four was the youngest prime minister during the French Revolution and the subsequent Napoleonic Wars. Pitt helped refine the position of prime minister in running the British government. Churchill admired his administrative innovations as well as his drive and energy. That Churchill's son, Randolph, shared Pitt's birthday was an added plus.

> *"One mark of a great man is the power of making lasting impressions upon the people he meets."*
> **Winston S. Churchill**

Churchill's introspection, values, and role models gave him the intellectual motivation necessary to be courageous when the moment arose.

ACTION THIS DAY

♦ Who are your heroes?

♦ What do you admire most about each hero?

♦ Which aspects of their lives have you emulated?

♦ Has emulating your heroes resulted in some successes? If so, what?

9

QUALITIES THAT CULTIVATE COURAGE—
TAKING ACTION

Courage is about overcoming fear and taking appropriate actions. Clarity of purpose enables a person to align his or her values which, when under attack, will result in action being taken.

Even Churchill was plagued with numerous fears: the fear of failure, shame, rejection, ridicule, disgrace, and making a mistake. Fear is a powerful force. It greatly influences how we think, feel, and act.

Fear is a primary emotion. However, it may be disguised by secondary emotions such as worry, anger, frustration, impatience, or dread. Thus, when a person feels threatened, a person may actually be experiencing fear in the form of these secondary emotions.

No one performs at his or her best when fear dominates a situation. A constant diet of strong apprehensions erodes one's capacity to function mentally and physically.

On the other hand, the presence of some concern may be essential to keep a person alert, sharp, and on one's toes.

Some people, like Churchill, seem to thrive in an environment of trepidation. His daring nature during World War II was honed by repeated exposures to shocking environments on battlefields in Cuba, in India (especially in what is now Pakistan), in the Sudan, in

South Africa, and in the trenches of the Western Front in World War I. He enjoyed visiting the front in France and Belgium during the Great War while he was First Lord of the Admiralty and later the Minister of Munitions. He also learned to fly when airplanes were primitive contraptions, and in the early days as Prime Minister flew to France when he might have been intercepted by Nazi fighters.

Courage is taking action despite fear. An important distinction is that fear is what you feel (an emotion) while courage is what you do (an action). The two can co-exist in time and space.

A study of Churchill's life and leadership reveals he employed a variety of courage-building strategies:

- **He did the thing he feared** and the fear lessened or went away, resulting in a tolerance to fear.

- **He served on military and political teams** that shared his fears.

- **He relished team rituals**—martial music, bagpipes, flags, uniforms, gestures (including his V for victory) to give him encouragement (which means to inspire with courage, spirit, or hope).

- In the military, **he trained and cross-trained.** The familiar can help to minimize the impact of fear.

- **He exercised self-discipline** by controlling his thoughts and emotions during frightful moments—keeping a stiff upper lip.

- **He used the power of humor**—smiling in the face of danger.

- **He partook in comfort food**—Churchill enjoyed good food (and alcohol), eaten on time and unhurriedly if possible.

- **He motivated himself** through his self-talk and visualization of the positive outcomes he sought.

Churchill's actions fell into two categories—those that were proactive and those that were reactive in nature. Whether he used one versus the other depended on the situation.

Churchill became Prime Minister in May, 1940. Later in the year and early into 1941, he started receiving Enigma decrypts from a captured German cypher machine that suggested that Hitler was going to violate his 1939 non-aggression pact with Stalin and the Soviet Union.

Churchill had an extreme dislike for Bolshevism and the Communists. He realized, however, that at the time Hitler was the greater danger both to Britain and to western civilization. He proactively (and courageously) sent messages to Stalin warning him of Hitler's treachery. Stalin ignored the messages. He even showed one message to Hitler to demonstrate to the Führer his good faith.

Hitler's three-and-a-half-million storm troopers invaded the Soviet Union across an eight-hundred-mile front from Finland to Romania on 22 June 1941. Churchill then reactively made overtures to Stalin now that they both had a common foe.

Both of Churchill's actions, the proactive one and the reactive one, were risky politically as well as subject to shame, ridicule, and failure. When asked why he reached out to a Communist leader who ordered the mass murder of tens of millions in the 1920s and 1930s, Churchill replied, "If Hitler invaded hell, I would make at least a favorable reference to the devil in the House of Commons."

Churchill acted courageously by taking action in four general ways: risk taking, boldness, decisiveness, and presence.

ACTION THIS DAY

◆ **What are your greatest personal and professional fears? How do you manage your fears? How successful have you been?**

◆ **What can you do to become more proactive? What is the cost to you for not being more proactive?**

TAKING ACTION 1—RISK TAKING

Risk is defined as the exposure to some peril, danger, or hazard and the possibility of loss or injury. While risk reduction, mitigation, and avoidance are cottage industries today, people during World War II understood that it was inherent in their fight for survival against the Nazis.

Churchill was an avowed risk taker. He used a variety of risk-assessment and management strategies to identify worst-case scenarios and to develop appropriate, balanced responses that lessened its impact.

> *"You have to run risks. There is a precipice on either side of you—a precipice of caution and a precipice of over daring."*
> **Winston S. Churchill**

Churchill's approach to risk included:

- **He exercised restraint and avoided being impulsive.** Churchill often struggled with his desire to get things done immediately and had to realize that patience in the present might save lives in the future.

- **He learned from mistakes.** Churchill had a phenomenal memory for facts, material he had read, and people he had met (especially if he might need them in the future). For example, in *The Gathering Storm*, he recalled a lesson of the 1915 Dardanelles fiasco by observing, "Never attempt to carry out a major and cardinal operation from a subordinate position."

Churchill lacked the authority needed to insist the attack on Turkish positions be continued. Hence, a naval action deteriorated into a nine-month army campaign with deadly results.

> *"Success cannot be guaranteed.*
> *There are no safe battles."*
> **Winston S. Churchill**

- **He embraced excellence, not perfection.** To be perfect meant not making any mistakes. Churchill saw that in war mistakes often happened. Perfection would paralyze performance and keep people from taking action. As Churchill observed, "The maxim 'nothing avails but perfection' may be spelt shorter: 'paralysis.'" On the other hand, excellence accepts some mistakes but relies on high standards of performance.

- **Churchill did not attempt to control the uncontrollable.** He knew it was pointless to attempt to control the reactions, opinions, or honesty of other people. He couldn't control world events such as Hitler's invasion of the Soviet Union. He couldn't control the weather, especially the weather just prior to the D-Day offensive. He hoped that by his words and deeds he might influence others and circumstances.

- **He was open to new ideas and actions.** Churchill was curious.

- **He was persistent and tenacious.** He simply refused to give up.

- **He danced with changing circumstances.** Nothing stays the same. Churchill learned to roll with the punches. If he got knocked down, he stood back up.

- **He was innovative in problem solving.** Churchill's fertile imagination regularly came up with unique and imaginative solutions. His probing questions often elicited new avenues of possibility.

Churchill grasped that balanced risk taking modulated the inherently dangerous environments in which he operated. Since risks can neither be avoided nor should they be irresponsibly pursued, Churchill used these strategies to lower his and Britain's exposure to losses and failure.

ACTION THIS DAY

♦ Are you more a risk-adverse individual or a risk taker? Why?

♦ How do you manage risk? Have you found ways to balance and reduce risks?

♦ Do you have a different risk threshold personally and professionally? Why?

TAKING ACTION 2—BOLDNESS

Courage sits dormant in some people. However, people can condition themselves to respond to future demands because courage is like a muscle. The more it is used, the stronger the muscle will become.

Winston Churchill's thoughts, words, and deeds over a lifetime of challenging situations gave him the mettle necessary to meet his greatest trial—being prime minister during the Second World War. He employed several boldness-building strategies before he was able to exercise command of Britain's fight for survival.

- **He stepped outside his physical, intellectual, and emotional comfort zones.** Churchill's participation in combat in several Victorian wars as well as his Cabinet level postings provided regular departures from his comfort zones.

- **He made change a challenge, not a curse.** Change, especially in warfare, is unavoidable. Churchill transformed change into an ally. When he orchestrated change, he felt more comfortable. He could accommodate surprise by not panicking and reserving judgment until he saw the problem more clearly. Churchill noted, "There is nothing wrong with change if it is in the right direction. To improve is to change. To be perfect [he meant "excellent"] is to change often."

- **He changed his perspective.** He routinely adopted an optimistic view of future events as opposed to a negative viewpoint. He committed himself proactively instead of procrastinating. He accepted risk instead of playing it safe. He committed to taking a stand instead of making an exit. He became a victor rather than a victim. In effect, Churchill chose how he would react to circumstances. He selected an empowering perspective instead of a discouraging one.

- **He competed in challenging situations by taking difficult assignments.** Throughout Churchill's military life, he routinely exposed himself to physical danger. As a politician, he took unpopular positions that held a possibility of ridicule. Neither the danger nor the ridicule dissuaded Churchill. That he willingly became prime minister during his nation's most perilous hour verifies this element.

- **He broadened his experience.** Churchill's successive Cabinet posts exposed him to the internecine political battles constantly being waged. He became a master in dealing in the Byzantine world of intrigue, distortion, deception, and party fratricide of British politics.

- **He developed sound judgment.** Churchill asked probing questions. He developed sound judgment by developing the discernment to identify genuine experts from pretenders. He essentially sought the answers to two questions: **1. So what?** That is, what is significant about this? **2. Now what?**

- **He critiqued both individual and team battles.** Churchill could act boldly because he always sought to improve. Therefore, his private critiques as well as his public ones centered on three questions: 1. What went right? 2. What when wrong? 3. What can be done differently next time?

Churchill also demonstrated a subtle form of boldness in the persuasiveness of his opinions when he was defending a political or military position. His rhetorical arguments were like incessant siege cannons pummeling a well-defended castle. By force of will, he usually prevailed.

John (Jock) Colville, Churchill's private secretary during both his terms as prime minister, observed about his boss, "His charm, his energy, the simplicity of his purpose, his unfailing sense of fun, and his complete absence of personal vanity—so rare in successful men—were the Secret Weapon which outmatched any that Hitler could produce."

ACTION THIS DAY

♦ How regularly do you step out of your physical, intellectual, and emotional comfort zones?

♦ How have you broadened your experience by taking a more difficult, complex, and challenging assignment?

TAKING ACTION 3—DECISIVENESS

Courageous people, like Winston Churchill, are decisive. He could not know beforehand whether his decisions were right or wrong or whether they came at the appropriate time. But Churchill had the courage to decide based on the best information he had available at the time. He did what he needed to do, and he let history pass judgment.

Churchill's behaviors concerning decision making indicated that he:

- **Was not afraid to make a decision**, if one were needed. Many of his choices were unpredictable, but his motivations were largely transparent. He also discerned unexpected distinctions others missed which reinforced the unpredictability of his choices.

- **Believed a decision was preferable to inaction**.

- **Saw the big picture** involving the problem.

- **Comprehended the nuances** contained in the details of the problem.

- **Accounted for the wild cards** of variance in performance, uncertainties in uncontrollable elements, and the unpredictability of risk.

- **Collaborated** with his staff and colleagues but made the final decision.

- **Was prepared to refine his decision** based on new information.

- **Took complete responsibility** for the decision whether it proved to be the right one or not.

Luck (or chance) plays a role in decision making. Some leaders are simply lucky. Subordinates tend to favor lucky leaders because their principal's luck may help them to survive a crisis or calamity. Churchill was such a leader. He escaped certain death on several occasions. He admitted, "Nothing in life is so exhilarating as to be shot at without result."

Churchill visited the battlefields in France and Belgium eleven times between becoming Minister of Munitions in July, 1917, and the end of the war in November, 1918. Several times he experienced enemy barrages and on one occasion shrapnel fell only five yards away. He was even present for the beginning of the great German counter-offensive on the Western Front in March, 1918. He survived all these. He was lucky!

Seneca the Younger asserted, "Luck is when preparation meets opportunity." And Churchill was routinely well prepared, especially when making rulings and defending them in the War Cabinet. Churchill concluded, "We have always to be on guard against being thrown off our course by chance and circumstance."

"Hasty work and premature decisions may lead to penalties out of all proportion to the issues immediately involved."
Winston S. Churchill

While it is not possible to know exactly what cognitive processes were going on in Churchill's mind as he reached a decision, he might have considered the following:

- **What was the challenge** to be overcome?

- **What were the various options** to solve the challenge?

- **What was the worst-case** solution?

- **What was the best-case**, highest-payoff solution?

- **What was the most likely outcome** for each solution?

- **Were there any force multipliers** in a solution?

- **Were there any wild cards** that were likely to come into play?

- **What was the most easily executed solution?**

- Based on the above, **what would be the best solution to the challenge?**

Churchill would have agreed with Admiral John Arbuthnot "Jacky" Fisher, his pre-World War I naval advisor and later First Sea Lord, who proclaimed his 3R's of warfare: "Ruthless, Relentless, and Remorseless."

Churchill had to make hard decisions in war. He ordered troops to fight to the last man (e.g., Calais and Singapore) and firebombed German cities (e.g., Hamburg and Dresden). He perceived, "For good or for ill, right or wrong, in war you must know what you want and what you mean and hurl your whole life and strength into it and accept all hazards inseparable from it."

ACTION THIS DAY

◆ Are you comfortable taking complete responsibility for a decision?

◆ What factors do you consider when making a decision?

TAKING ACTION 4—PRESENCE

Winston Churchill's example of courage has been impressive and well documented. He was renowned for being where the action was. He liked to see things for himself first hand—troop positions and training centers, coastal and antiaircraft defenses, dockyards and military bases, and bombed cities and towns.

Nowhere was Churchill's presence more important than in London during the Blitz. He was typically found examining bomb damage after a raid. He encouraged Londoners and shared their sorrows. He was not afraid to shed a tear in public. He genuinely cared about his countrymen.

Today's leaders can benefit from the example Churchill set throughout his military and political careers.

- **He made difficult decisions.**

- **He took balanced risks.**

- **He led from the front, not the rear.**

- He was seen by his countrymen and military forces as **sharing their dangers** and showing compassion for their losses.

- **He did not confine himself to the solutions of the past.**

- **He set the standard** for honesty and integrity by taking morally appropriate actions.

- **He responded to a crisis** with strength, confidence and poise.

- **He motivated** his followers with enthusiasm and encouragement during periods of adversity, hardship, and suffering.

- **He could make the distinction between courage** and its absence. When he recognized that courage was missing, he filled in the gap.

- **He kept hope alive.**

By seeing events himself, Churchill derived unfiltered information and observations. An objective, first-hand observation is worth scores of second- or third-hand anecdotal reports. In addition, his physical presence rallied both troops and countrymen. A leader must be seen by his followers. Churchill also preferred meeting key political and military players face to face.

Churchill wanted to accompany the troops ashore in Normandy on D-Day. While he claimed he would get a much better measure of the battle's success, others (including General Eisenhower) deemed him too important to risk himself that way. Eventually, it was King George VI who stopped him by insisting that he, too, would join the troops. Churchill reluctantly relented.

> *"There is great hope provided action*
> *is taken worthy of the opportunity."*
> **Winston S. Churchill**

If Churchill's presence were a demonstration of his physical courage, his stand on principled issues revealed his moral presence. He did not shy away from controversial issues.

For example, as President of the Board of Trade (1908-1910), he instituted minimum wages, labor dispute mediation, job placement systems, and removed unhealthy working conditions. As Home Secretary (1910-1911), he introduced prison reforms as well as widows' and orphans' pensions. Churchill did most of the legwork in 1908 for unemployment and health insurance that Lloyd George ushered in by 1911.

Churchill also supported the Balfour Declaration in 1917 regarding the establishment of a Jewish National Home in Palestine. As Colonial Secretary, he reaffirmed the right of Jews to their ancestral lands in a 1922 White Paper.

These stands were unpopular with the Tories. Churchill was regarded as a liberal reformer (a radical to the Tories) and an architect of the future welfare state in Britain. Churchill's moral convictions, nonetheless, gave him the courage to support what he thought was the correction of social injustices.

ACTION THIS DAY

♦ How do you get unfiltered information about your subordinates' work?

♦ How do you keep hope alive for others?

DETERMINATION

10

DETERMINATION

Churchill pursued compelling challenges with a vision sourced by discernment, passion, and innovation. Then he took those first few critical steps with courage based on his clarity of purpose and action. Finally, he continued to strive toward his vision by following through with determination.

Perseverance involves maintaining, and possibly even accelerating, momentum until the vision is achieved. Waiting in the wings are multiple obstacles that, if not managed, will impede the journey to the vision.

Self-doubt steals more dreams than the worst thief. "We have met the enemy and it's us," claims the comic strip character, Pogo. And if self-doubt were not enough, Churchill comprehended that action begets adversity, yet "difficulties mastered are opportunities won."

Breakdowns, that is, totally unexpected events, proliferate. These might be naturally occurring obstacles or man-made calamities. They might be an error in judgment or a purposeful act of injustice. They may be something outside one's awareness in the "did not know that one did not know" category.

Churchill approached adversity and breakdowns as if they were inconveniences, not show stoppers. In wartime, ships were sunk, armies captured, and cities bombed. He tended to use adversity as an opportunity to recommit to his intended course of action. If the breakdown were serious, Churchill might offer words of encouragement or hope in a Parliamentary speech or a broadcast on the BBC.

> *"When we face with a steady eye the difficulties which lie before us, we may derive new confidence from remembering those we have already overcome."*
> **Winston S. Churchill**

Churchill reflected that the path to the "broad sunlit uplands" would be cluttered with obstacles and distractions. Deep chasms would separate his countrymen from their dreams.

At times like those, they needed to remember their vision of victory. They needed to keep moving forward with courage. And determination would get them there if they never gave in.

Determination found life in two Churchillian leadership elements: motivation and resilience.

ACTION THIS DAY

♦ How do you deal with breakdowns?

♦ How do you motivate others in the face of adversity?

11

QUALITIES THAT DEEPEN DETERMINATION—
MOTIVATION

Churchill realized that genuine motivation was sourced from the inside out. External events, people, incentives, and inducements might influence how a person acted, but only the individual could control how he or she responded.

Churchill was a self-starter and prime mover. He did not rely on the opinions of others for motivation. He never lost his focus and clearly saw his goal. He clothed himself in courage to defend himself from fear. He surrounded himself with possibility people, not pessimists. He ran his own race.

Motivation is a gift given by a leader to his followers. It is born out of love and generosity. In the early days of the Second World War, Churchill's words, presence, and actions infused his countrymen with dedication and resolve. He also gave heart to millions of other people in America and Europe who were afraid of Nazi aggression.

> *"No one knows till he tries how much influence one convinced and well-informed person can exert upon those with whom he comes in contact in the ordinary round of daily life."*
> **Winston S. Churchill**

Churchill harnessed the powers of motivation in four ways: self-confidence, tenacity, discipline, and industry.

ACTION THIS DAY

♦ What is the source of your motivation?

♦ You can motivate others only when you are fed and recharged. How do you recharge so you can motivate others?

♦ How would others characterize your motivation—a gift born out of love and generosity or a duty you must perform?

♦ How important it is to motivate others?

MOTIVATION 1—SELF-CONFIDENCE

Churchill's unbounded self-confidence was the fuel that propelled him in challenging, difficult situations. It was seen throughout his adult life both on the battlefield and in his government service. He manifested this self-confidence via:

- **Knowing himself.** He appreciated his ability to perform in dangerous, high-pressure, and unknown situations and environments. He accepted his superlative talents: his memory for details, his imagination for unique solutions, and his mastery of oratory and the written word. He stood firm in his values and principles.

> *"The threat of adversity is a necessary factor in stimulating self-reliance."*
> **Winston S. Churchill**

- **Reframing negativity into positive opportunities.** He focused on goals and upbeat expectations. He thought optimistically.

- **Remembering past successes and victories.** He recalled how he had overcome difficulties. Accordingly, he prepared to triumph over past deficiencies. He increased his knowledge base.

Churchill's self-confidence was reflected in his ebullient demeanor. He took time to enjoy food, company, and conversation (mostly his own). He was always well dressed.

> *"I have no fear of the future. Let us go forward into its mysteries, let us tear aside the veils which hide it from our eyes, and let us move onward with confidence and courage."*
> Winston S. Churchill

ACTION THIS DAY

♦ On a scale of 1 to 10 (10 is the highest), how self-confident are you?

♦ What does your self-confidence allow you to do? If you had more self-confidence, what could you do that you're not doing now?

♦ How can you build your self-confidence?

♦ Do you have a victory log listing past successes? Consulting this during new challenges helps you gain additional self-confidence.

MOTIVATION 2—TENACITY

Tenacity symbolized the pointed end of the spear of Churchill's motivation. Tenacity was Churchill's brand personified by the defiant bulldog, the jaunty V for victory, and the cigar.

Tenacity is extreme persistence. It manifested itself in Churchill's thoughts, words, and deeds. He relentlessly pursued his objectives regardless of the weight of possible defeat or failure.

Churchill's tenacity was the product of:

- **Being prepared** for fear, evil, danger, and the unknown.

- **Going the extra mile**, that is, doing more than was required to achieve the desired outcome. Churchill continued to "pester, nag, and bite."

- **Not leaving follow-through to chance.**

- **Being guided by his established values and principles.**

> *"Never give in! Never give in! Never, never, never, never—in nothing great or small, large or petty—never give in except to convictions of honor and good sense. Never yield to force; never yield to the apparently overwhelming might of the enemy."*
> **Winston S. Churchill**

- **Maintaining momentum of action.** He sought to move forward boldly, not fearfully or timidly. Churchill would have agreed with General

Douglas MacArthur who decried, "Councils of war breed timidity and defeatism."

Churchill's tenacity also applied to his powers of persuasion. He could be irresistibly charming or, if necessary, particularly forceful. This illuminates the realization that a strength taken to excess becomes a weakness. Self-confidence remains a vital trait for any leader. Overconfidence, however, may lead to overextended judgments and actions.

ACTION THIS DAY

♦ How do you mentally prepare for fear and surprises?

♦ How can you be even more proactive in anticipating events?

MOTIVATION 3—DISCIPLINE

Churchill respected that discipline was the fountainhead of success.

For Churchill, discipline took the form of mental toughness. He dedicated himself to achieving outcomes that he believed were noble, honorable, and necessary. He was obedient to himself by driving his own train. He avoided merely being a passenger of circumstances, opinions, and chance.

> *"The bond of discipline is subtle and sensitive. It may be as tense as steel or as brittle as glass."*
> **Winston S. Churchill**

Churchill was disciplined by:

- **Controlling his emotions** to harness all his time and energy on actions that moved the ball down the field.

- **Exercising self-control** by the power of his will.

- **Possessing an intense laser focus** on the desired outcomes.

- **Filtering the circumstances** impinging upon him through the lens of his objectives.

- **Ignoring the inner voice** that told him to relax, to rest, to postpone, to seek pleasure, to avoid pain, and to opt for near-term gratification over long-term reward.

- **Transforming breakdowns (negatives) into breakthroughs (positives).** When obstacles arose, he changed direction but did not alter his decision to pursue a course of action.

- **Conditioning himself** to withstand hardships and privation. He was comfortable being uncomfortable when it came to winning the war.

- **Meeting and achieving** personal and national goals.

- **Seeing sacrifices as necessary** and as a barometer for his commitment to success and victory.

- **Possessing an uncompromising sense of duty, dedication, and drive.** He did what he said he would do. No ambiguity! No equivocation!

- **Using a step-by-step approach to move closer to his goals.**

Discipline gave Churchill the mental momentum to persevere despite setbacks and defeats. It helped him keep his disappointments and frustrations at bay.

ACTION THIS DAY

♦ On a scale of 1 to 10 (10 being the most), how disciplined are you?

♦ What would be the impact on your personal and professional life if you were more disciplined?

♦ What things could you do to become more disciplined?

MOTIVATION 4—INDUSTRY

Churchill's numerous accomplishments were extraordinary! His voluminous books, speeches, articles, instructions, memoranda, papers, notes, letters, meetings, and even oil paintings reveal a man blessed with an amazing capacity for work. Each of these efforts represents a substantial investment of time and energy.

Churchill's personal productivity while occupying major Cabinet positions during both world wars reveals a leader who demonstrated both effectiveness and efficiency. He clearly was an expert at time mastery.

> *"Time is neutral; but it can be made an ally of those who seize it and can use it to the full."*
> **Winston S. Churchill**

Churchill left an extensive record that documented his thoughts, words, and actions. He also kept records of his personal and professional schedule and visitors. Diaries, journals, and memoirs of his personal staff, colleagues, and contemporaries further report on Churchill's prodigious output.

Churchill's "wilderness years," while he was in political exile from 1929 to 1939, gave him a unique break. He had an opportunity for reflection and a period of personal regrowth as well as for a remarkable period of productivity.

He authored eleven books (including his *History of the English-Speaking People* later published in the 1950s) and four volumes of speeches. He also painted over two hundred landscape oil paintings. This period helped him recharge and gave him a solid foundation upon which he could rely during the subsequent sterner days of the Second World War.

Churchill's industry revealed that he:

- **Was willing to work**, taking whatever time necessary to accomplish his duty. He was conscientious, being especially diligent and vigilant in actions involving national defense.

- **Employed traditional time-management techniques** such as planning, scheduling, and keeping to-do lists. He delegated to his private secretaries and staff the charge of keeping him on time and up to date.

- **Delegated** to military leaders and Cabinet ministers the authority (but not the responsibility) to perform vital assignments.

- **Did not procrastinate** regardless of how unpleasant or complex the work was. Lazy, bored, and idle were words that did not apply to Churchill. He lived "Action This Day" and his subordinates did so, too.

- Had his staff **eliminate distractions and interruptions** when and where possible.

- **Was assertive in his communications** to ensure people understood clearly what was asked of them.

> *"Strength is granted to us all when*
> *we are needed to serve great causes."*
> **Winston S. Churchill**

- **Prioritized to-do lists** by their urgency and importance. The initial years of the Second World War were predominately both urgent and important. Churchill was most adept at leading during a crisis. As British military forces grew and the invasion threat of England lessened, he could tackle more tasks that were important but not urgent. Churchill might have also been aware of and used the Pareto Principle that stated that 80% of the effects come from 20% of the causes.

- **Used his time wisely.** Despite the heavy pace of activity, he avoided overscheduling that would leave him exhausted. He often needed blocks of time to write and prepare for a speech. Churchill observed, "Energy of mind does not depend on energy of body . . . Energy should be exercised and not exhausted."

- **Believed hard work contributed to victory.**

ACTION THIS DAY

♦ On a scale of 1 to 10 (10 being the most), how industrious are you?

♦ If you were more industrious, what could you accomplish in your personal and professional life that you're presently not accomplishing?

♦ What things can you do to become more industrious?

12

QUALITIES THAT DEEPEN DETERMINATION— RESILIENCE

Winston Churchill was an amazingly resilient person in his ability to adapt to adversity. He possessed the fortitude to endure trials and tribulations in the pursuit of victory. He regularly bounced back from obstacles, traumas, defeats, stresses, and failures. He possessed a positive, optimistic attitude and envisioned an empowering future.

Churchill derived strength from his realistic vision, from compelling reasons for attaining his objective, from success-oriented values, and from a strong sense of purpose. He directed his time and energy to actions he could control or significantly influence. He managed his emotions and exercised impulse control. He pivoted with agility when he encountered setbacks, disappointments, and surprises.

Churchill saw crises as an opportunity to excel, not retreat. He fathomed that failure was feedback for fostering future success. While failures were never sought, when they came, he learned from them and continued to move forward. He would look at every situation and ask, "What's needed next?"

Churchill's resilient strength grew from three elements: flexibility, patience, and self-renewal.

ACTION THIS DAY

♦ How have you demonstrated resilience in your personal and professional life? What adversities have you experienced?

♦ How did overcoming adversity cause you to grow?

♦ How do you deal with failure? How do you deal with the failure of others? Are you the coach or the critic?

RESILENCE 1—FLEXIBILITY

Churchill demonstrated an uncanny ability to adapt to change. Flexibility gave him the momentum to press forward when he encountered the unexpected.

Flexibility began in Churchill's mind. He was open to new ideas and ways of doing things, not tied to established practices.

> *"The best method for acquiring flexibility is to have three or four plans for all the probable contingencies, all worked out with the utmost detail. Then it is much easier to switch from one to the other as and when the cat jumps."*
> **Winston S. Churchill**

Churchill's flexibility grew out of suspending judgment about how to reach his outcomes. Rather than assigning values such as right or wrong, good or bad, he classified alternative approaches objectively. He considered a spectrum of options ranging from the most optimistic consequence to the most undesirable result. As Churchill noted, "One must remember that a ship may start out in one direction and turn off in another."

Most people are change adverse because change engenders the fear of the unknown. Churchill knew how to adjust to shifting circumstances. To move forward with a vision meant change would be necessary.

Churchill positioned himself to anticipate change and thereby minimized being surprised by it. His ability to visualize new situations grew out of his uncanny historical perspective. He observed historical trends and parallels that gave him insights into unfolding events. Additionally, he learned to pivot when circumstances changed.

"I am certainly not one of those who need to be prodded. In fact if anything, I am a prod."
Winston S. Churchill

Churchill was willing to discard approaches, policies, attitudes, beliefs, and biases that were no longer true in the white light of reality.

ACTION THIS DAY

♦ How flexible are you in adapting to change? Is change more a curse or a challenge for you?

♦ How do you help others to adapt to change? Is this leadership by example?

♦ How often are you proactive versus reactive with respect to change?

RESILIENCE 2—PATIENCE

Winston Churchill accepted that regardless of his desires, most things proceeded at their own rate. He realistically felt, "Fearthought is futile worrying over what cannot be averted or will probably never happen."

Churchill did not confuse patience with inactivity, passivity, procrastination, or idleness. Patience meant that some things simply cannot be rushed. He recognized that delaying immediate enjoyment resulted in an even greater subsequent reward.

> *"We must not lose patience,*
> *and we must not lose hope."*
> **Winston S. Churchill**

Churchill was not patient with his immediate staff, his military leaders, and Cabinet ministers when it came to obtaining information he needed to make a decision. He was, however, not mean, petty, or vindictive. He grasped that implementing new military technology, as well as planning and executing military operations, took time. He observed, "Patience, however, and good temper accomplish much."

Churchill was mindful that:

- **Successful leaders tend to be patient, uncomplaining, and cheerful.**

- **Courageous people are patiently open minded** as they interact with other people.

- **Good ideas are frequently not adopted immediately.**

- **Courageous leaders are rarely impulsive.**

- **Courageous leaders create an open environment based on mutual trust that encourages discussion.**

- **Patient leaders want their teams to think from as many different perspectives as possible.**

- **Problem solvers must take the time to generate as many options and potential solutions as possible for the decision makers.**

Throughout his life, Churchill had tests of patience, character, and endurance. He met these with fortitude and resolve as well as with grace, poise, and courage. His years of preparation made his years of achievement memorable. His service and experience seasoned him into a statesman possessing much-needed wisdom for a world in turmoil.

Churchill's personal mission was steeped in patience. This was because in war, few things happen according to schedule. This mission is best described in words Churchill originally developed for a war memorial in France following the First World War. Unfortunately, his evocative words were declined. That allowed Churchill to use them later for the moral of his six-volume war memoirs, *The Second World War*.

> *"In War: Resolution*
> *In Defeat: Defiance*
> *In Victory: Magnanimity*
> *In Peace: Good Will"*
> Winston S. Churchill

ACTION THIS DAY

♦ On a scale of 1 to 10 (10 is the highest), how patient are you? Why?

♦ Your impatience may be sourced in fear. What things are you apprehensive about? Is there a better way to communicate these concerns to others instead of being impatient?

♦ What tests of patience, character, or endurance have you faced? How have these helped you to be a better leader?

RESILIENCE 3—SELF-RENEWAL

Winston Churchill survived and thrived in environments dominated by stress. These included combat, bombings, power politics, fear of invasion, and being shot down or torpedoed while traveling to strategic conferences.

The pace of the Second World War and Churchill's punishing schedule certainly stressed his sixty-five-year-old body. During the war, he basically only worked and slept. During his waking hours, he was thoroughly devoted to his work. Meals became working meetings. Journeys by car, train, ship, and plane were opportunities to meet and discuss important matters with his subordinates or to dictate instructions and memoranda.

Churchill took a ninety-minute power nap each afternoon followed by a second bath. These energized him to work from after supper until the early hours of the morning. He could accomplish a day-and-a-half's-worth of work each day. His extraordinary energy and vitality wore out much younger military and political colleagues who worked more conventional hours.

> *"Change is the master key. A man can wear out a particular part of his mind by continually using it and tiring it, just the same way he can wear out the elbows of his coat."*
> **Winston S. Churchill**

Food and drink became stress relievers for Churchill. Good food fortified him and gave him the sustenance to direct all his mind, body, and spirit to winning the war. Alcoholic libations relaxed him. Churchill once admitted, "All I can say is that I have taken more out of alcohol than alcohol has taken out of me."

Clementine Churchill ("Clemmie" or his beloved "Cat"), his wife and confidant, was Churchill's anchor in a sea of crisis. She once advised him not to return home from the trenches on the Western Front during World War I too prematurely lest it negatively impact his subsequent political career. "Patience is the only grace you need," was her guidance.

Some of Churchill's inner circle of friends, such as Brendan Bracken, Max Beaverbrook, and Frederick Lindemann (the "Prof"), allowed Churchill to vent without his words being recorded for posterity. These friends became another stress-relief outlet for him.

Churchill loved animals. Over his life, he enjoyed cats, dogs, Golden Orfe (fish), a budgerigar (common parakeet), black swans, and race horses. He admitted, "Dogs look up to you, cats look down on you. Give me a pig! He looks you in the eye and treats you as an equal."

Painting was Churchill's favorite pastime and hobby. He began painting oil landscapes after being forced to resign from the Admiralty in 1915. Due to the demanding nature of the Second World War, Churchill took time to paint only once, in Marrakech, Morocco, in 1943.

While traveling by warship to America, Churchill relaxed from round-the-clock discussions and planning conferences by watching an evening movie in the wardroom (e.g., the 1941 movie, *That Hamilton Woman* was his favorite), reading a novel (e.g., C.S.

Forester's, *Captain Hornblower*), or playing cards (e.g., Bezique).

Singing ditties from Gilbert and Sullivan operas and reciting poems by Rudyard Kipling helped Churchill relax. His phenomenal memory allowed him to recall long passages from books and poems he learned as a schoolboy.

Between the wars, Churchill also relaxed by creating lakes, ponds, gardens, and brick walls at Chartwell, his magnificent country home in Kent. He became a rather proficient bricklayer. However, he never exercised. He claimed, "I get my exercise serving as pall-bearer to my many friends who exercised all their lives."

Churchill successfully balanced a hurried, pressure-filled life with self-renewal activities that allowed him to function effectively and efficiently. As he noted, "We lived very simply—but with all the essentials of life well understood and provided for—hot baths, cold champagne, new peas and old brandy."

ACTION THIS DAY

♦ **On a scale of 1 to 10 (10 is the highest), how stressful is your personal life and separately, your work life?**

♦ **How do you relieve stress in your life?**

VICTORY

13

VICTORY

Victory has a clear definition: defeating or triumphing over an opponent or an enemy. It also means winning or achieving success in some endeavor.

Hitler sourced his identity in war. Churchill sourced his in victory. Andrew Roberts believed that, "Hitler was a charismatic leader while Churchill was an inspirational one." Hitler was a revolutionary tyrant. Churchill was a constitutional servant. (Churchill called himself "a Parliamentarian and House of Commons man.")

For Churchill, the alternative to victory in the Second World War was surrender, slavery, or death, none of which was an acceptable option. Churchill believed, "Once you are so unfortunate as to be drawn into a war, no price is too great to pay for an early and victorious peace."

Churchill never wavered from his single-minded pursuit of victory. He would have agreed with General Douglas MacArthur, "In war there is no substitute for victory." Churchill believed that a nation ought not expend its blood and treasure in conflict unless it sought to win.

Churchill understood the stark, raw realities of war, especially realizing that "both sides think they have a chance of winning." He observed combat first-hand as in three Victorian wars and again in the trenches of the First World War. He personally witnessed the cruel loss of life during the London Blitz as well as the destruction of homes and buildings (including the ruins of the House of Commons, which was bombed in May, 1941).

Churchill observed, "The utility of war even to the victor may in most cases be an illusion. Certainly all wars of every kind will be destitute of any positive advantage . . . but war itself, if ever it comes, will not be an illusion—even a single bullet will be found real enough."

When a person succeeds and achieves a vision, it does not imply other people are defeated or disadvantaged. Bringing better quality products and services to the market, for example, represents a mutually beneficial arrangement for both the supplier and the customer.

In the case of using the Churchill factors, victory takes on an expanded meaning. Achieving victory can mean victory over ignorance, victory over hunger, victory over injustice, victory over illness and disease, victory over poverty, or victory over fear. These are issues worthy of combatting with vision, courage, and determination until final triumphs usher in a new era of truth, liberty, peace, and prosperity.

Winston Churchill shared his hopes for humanity with, "If the human race wishes to have a prolonged and indefinite period of material prosperity, they have only got to behave in a peaceful and helpful way towards one another, and science will do for them all that they wish and more than they can dream . . .

". . . Nothing is final. Change is unceasing and it is likely that mankind has a lot more to learn before it comes to its journey's end . . .

". . . We might even find ourselves in a few years moving along a smooth causeway of peace and plenty instead of roaming around on the rim of Hell . . . Thus we may by patience, courage, and in orderly progression reach the shelter of a calmer and kindlier age."

What was Churchill's greatest legacy? It was his example as a man and as a leader of men and women. With vision, courage, and determination, he bequeathed us not only hope but victory.

ACTION THIS DAY

◆ **Where in your life are you victorious?**

◆ **How can you be more victorious?**

14

EPILOGUE: HIS FINEST HOUR AND YOURS

Winston Churchill's charismatic leadership developed during his extensive military and political service. By the time he was prime minister in 1940, his leadership reflexes were spontaneous and intuitive. He seamlessly synergized vision, courage, and determination to achieve the outcomes he sought. With them he became a heroic war leader, a brilliant strategist, and a respected statesman.

While historians may disagree as to Churchill's success as a leader and his judgment as a strategic thinker, it defies credibility that Edward Halifax, Clement Attlee, or Stafford Cripps could have done a better job as prime minister. David Howarth believed, "Many of those who write about history like to seem wiser than those who made history."

"Criticism is easy;
achievement is more difficult."
Winston S. Churchill

Churchill attended Harrow, an independent school for boys that covered the middle school and high school grades. The boys studied Macaulay as a way of being introduced to poetry and history as well as to important values like sacrifice and courage.

In 1888 Churchill memorized and recited 1,200 lines of Macaulay's *Lays of Ancient Rome*, winning a school-wide prize as a demonstration of his extraordinary memory. One portion of the poem was perhaps the fountainhead of Churchill's later vision.

In *Horatius*, the first poem in the *Lays*, we learn about how in 508 BC Horatius prevented the invading Etruscan army from crossing the west end of the Sublician Bridge over the Tiber and sacking the poorly defended Rome. He was the Captain of the Gate, and his actions saved Rome. Here's the call to action in Macaulay's poem:

> **But the Consul's brow was sad,**
> **   And the Consul's speech was low,**
> **And darkly looked he at the wall,**
> **   And darkly at the foe.**
> **"Their van will be upon us**
> **   Before the bridge goes down;**
> **And if they once may win the bridge,**
> **   What hope to save the town?"**

> **Then out spake brave Horatius,**
> **   The Captain of the Gate:**
> **"To every man upon this earth**
> **   Death cometh soon or late.**
> **And how can man die better**
> **   Than facing fearful odds,**
> **For the ashes of his fathers,**
> **   And the temples of his gods."**

Horatius made a lasting impression on the thirteen-year-old Churchill, who already admired his great hero ancestor, the Duke of Marlborough, for saving England at a critical moment.

In 1891, three years after his prize-winning performance, Churchill commented to a schoolmate, "This country will be subjected somehow to a tremendous invasion, by what means I do not know, but I tell you I shall be in command of the defenses of London and I shall save London and England from disaster."

The fulfillment of Churchill's vision from 1940 to 1945 was fortified by half a century of service in the British Army, his membership in Parliament, and his holding of multiple Cabinet posts in the British government especially during periods of crisis.

The British reversal in Norway precipitated the fall of Neville Chamberlain's government. Although the Foreign Secretary, Lord Edward Halifax, was the obvious successor, he did not think he could be effective as prime minister given his position in the House of Lords and the opposition from the Labour Party. While King George VI favored Halifax (as did Tory party leaders), it fell to Churchill to form and lead a new coalition government on 10 May 1940.

> *"I felt as if I were walking with Destiny,*
> *and that all my past life had been but a*
> *preparation for this hour and for this trial."*
> **Winston S. Churchill**

The last three weeks in May represented a tremendous challenge for a new leader assuming command of a nation at war. The unimaginable demands on Churchill tried his patience and taxed his strength. They also required him to radiate both optimism and flexibility that his government would set the right course to follow. He faced challenges head-on with grit and patriotism.

Churchill's staff was wary of their new boss due primarily to their established loyalty to his predecessor, Neville Chamberlain. Churchill was not initially regarded very highly by those who idolized Chamberlain. Over time, however, Churchill's industry and discipline convinced them that their earlier opinions of him were incorrect.

> *"I have nothing to offer but*
> *blood, toil, tears, and sweat."*
> **Winston S. Churchill**

The men of Munich (Chamberlain, Halifax, and other aristocratic appeasers) thought that Hitler might be amenable to a negotiated peace. Regardless of Hitler's record of deceit and brutality in Austria, Czechoslovakia, Poland, Denmark, Norway, Holland, Belgium, Luxembourg, and France, prominent leaders in Britain felt they could now trust the "Bohemian Corporal." Churchill held otherwise.

Churchill saw the big picture as he surveyed the amazing speed with which Hitler steamrolled other European nations. He did not need historical perspective to know that Britain was next on the Nazi invasion docket. Churchill's top priority was to fight until Britain achieved victory over the Teutonic tyrant. This became his focus both during the first three weeks of his government and until he finally grasped this goal five years later.

While Machiavellian intrigue and infighting stalked the corridors of Whitehall, the British Expeditionary Force in France and Belgium was suffering massive setbacks. Soon the BEF found itself in the sands of Dunkirk, destroying its guns, tanks, trucks, and ammunition before hoping to escape to England. The Luftwaffe strafed and bombed the beleaguered troops, wounding and killing many.

Churchill thought that perhaps only 50,000 of the BEF could be saved. (More than 330,000 Allied troops were eventually rescued because ordinary Englishmen launched small boats to bring them home.)

Churchill tried to rally the French leaders who were reluctant to fight and who favored a separate peace with Hitler. Despite great dangers, he even flew to France three times during this three-week time frame to encourage them.

In neutral America, President Franklin Roosevelt was suspicious of Churchill. He received a steady diet of pessimism from his ambassador to Britain, Joseph Kennedy (father of the future president), who believed that Churchill would be forced to surrender. Churchill, however, cultivated an alliance with FDR hoping to convince the American that Britain would fight on and would never surrender. The two leaders communicated regularly. Roosevelt soon learned to appreciate Churchill's boldness, enthusiasm, and convictions. Unfortunately for Britain, it would be another year and a half before America entered the war, and he realized they needed America to prevail.

Although Italy was tilting into the Nazi camp, Halifax still believed that Mussolini might serve as a go-between in negotiating a British peace accord with Hitler. He continued to press Churchill to reach some diplomatic agreement that would take Britain out of Hitler's crosshairs.

It was believed that such an arrangement might include loss of Britain's navy (what Hitler similarly planned when he conquered France) as well as loss of its strategic ports in Suez, Gibraltar, and Malta (if

Mussolini got his way by serving as an intermediary). Despite all the pressures from within his own government and the events taking place in Europe, Churchill would not pursue any peace terms with Hitler.

To add to Churchill's trials, if Halifax and Chamberlain resigned from the War Cabinet, a national crisis would erupt. In that case, Churchill might be forced to resign, and the King would invite Halifax to form a government. (Some even thought former Liberal Prime Minister David Lloyd George, now seventy-seven and an admirer of Hitler, might take the reins of government.) Halifax was a close friend of the King, but over time Churchill demonstrated that he would protect British interests more resolutely than Halifax.

Finally, on May 28th, Churchill refused to give way to Halifax's peace initiative. He had built a dominant position in the War Cabinet and a consensus in the full or Outer Cabinet (twenty-five members) that Britain would prefer to go down fighting instead of falling into Hitler's outstretched hand. Churchill in a grave and sonorous voice told his colleagues, "If this long island story of ours is to end at last, let it end only when each one of us lies choking in his own blood upon the ground."

"Our success must depend first upon our unity, then on our courage and endurance."
Winston S. Churchill

Churchill's first three weeks as prime minister could not have been more demanding for him! He was a man of uncompromising fearlessness. He tenaciously refused to yield to political expediency or to military might. He stopped Britain from negotiating away its freedom without a fight. No nation or leader could have stopped or defeated Hitler in 1940. Winston Churchill, however, never gave in. He never gave in to Halifax. He never gave in to Hitler. He never gave in. Never!

It all came down to Churchill's valiant words, prescient judgment, raw courage, and dogged determination. British and Commonwealth warriors fought on for another year and a half. Churchill encouraged innovations that helped Britain maintain air superiority which prevented the Nazis from successfully invading the home island.

> *"Never in the field of human conflict*
> *was so much owed by so many to so few."*
> **Winston S. Churchill**

Churchill presided over several military disasters until the end of 1942. The loss of the battleship, *Prince of Wales*, as well as the fall of Singapore and Tobruk, gave Churchill's political opponents much fuel to demand his resignation. Yet Churchill was not the architect of Britain's military unpreparedness nor was any other nation capable of standing up to Hitler's might. Churchill's self-confidence, although challenged, was met by his simplicity of purpose, clearly communicated with eloquence, resolution, and defiance.

Churchill knew that sending tanks and aircraft to North Africa was a risk, but British shipping depended on the Suez Canal. In addition, Churchill, like Lincoln, struggled to find a general with enough fighting spirit to win victories on the battlefield against both the Italians and General Erwin Rommel, the Desert Fox.

Churchill watched as the war unfolded on the high seas in the treacherous North Atlantic, in the forbidding Arctic, and in the perilous Mediterranean. America played the major role of engaging and finally defeating the Japanese in the daunting Pacific.

The planned Allied invasion of Normandy involved Churchill's alliance with Roosevelt, General Eisenhower, and the British and American Combined Chiefs of Staff. He also collaborated with teams of scientists and military experts who created innovations that ensured victory on D-Day. Once again, one cannot imagine a Halifax or an Attlee being the right person to lead Britain during any of these trials.

Some historians ascribe Churchill's finest hour to his first three weeks as prime minister. Others regard it as the year and a half that Britain fought alone.

Hitler invaded Russia on 22 June 1941, and Japan attacked Pearl Harbor on 7 December the same year brought Russia and America respectively into the war. The end of the war in Europe (8 May 1945) marked the fulfillment of Churchill's predestined vision.*

Thus, in much the same way that Churchill's Nobel Prize for Literature in 1953 was for the entire body of his work, his remarkable service during the entire war can justifiably be called "his finest hour."

****

In his last great speech to the House of Commons in 1955 (Churchill remained in Parliament until 1964), Churchill urged, "There is time and hope if we combine patience and courage . . . The day may dawn when fair

141

play, love for one's fellow-men, respect for justice and freedom, will enable tormented generations to march forth serene and triumphant from the hideous epoch in which we have to dwell. Meanwhile, never flinch, never weary, never despair."

****

The Churchill factors offer leaders today a tractable approach for achieving victory and success. With discernment, passion, and innovation, you will be able to develop a compelling vision. With clarity of purpose and action, you will meet obstacles and challenges with courage. And with motivation and resilience, you will press forward with determination until you finally achieve your vision.

"Give us the tools, and we will finish the job."
Winston S. Churchill

Vision, courage, and determination gave Churchill what he needed to emerge victoriously from the most devastating war in human history. His remarkable leadership revealed his finest hour.

Churchill's strategy for success embodied in the Churchill factors will give you, too, the means to create your finest hour!

*Churchill was subsequently voted out of office as prime minister and gave up his post on 26 July 1945. The war in the Pacific ended on 2 September 1945.

THE CHURCHILL FACTORS

VISION

Discernment

Priorities/Focus
Big Picture/Details
Historical Perspective
Simplicity

Passion

Enthusiasm/Exuberance
Optimism
Alliances
Clear Communications

Innovation

Trust
Creativity
Courage

COURAGE

Clarity of Purpose

Introspection
Values
Benchmarking Heroes

Taking Action

Risk Taking
Boldness
Decisiveness
Presence

DETERMINATION

Motivation

Self-Confidence
Tenacity
Discipline
Industry

Resilience

Flexibility
Patience
Self-Renewal

VICTORY

143

POSTSCRIPT

Many good academic approaches to leadership exist, but the Churchill factors were developed by one man who was himself a leader. He tested them in the trenches both in combat and in peacetime. By the time the Second World War began, he had refined them like tempered steel and was able to translate his vision of victory to his nation and to the world. His personal courage ignited his countrymen. And his determination in the face of insurmountable obstacles caused Englishmen to rally again and again when they thought all was lost.

In his celebrated work, *The Seven Pillars of Wisdom*, T. E. Lawrence observed, "All men dream but not equally. Those who dream by night in the dusty recesses of their minds wake in the day to find that it was vanity, but the dreamers of the day are dangerous men for they may act their dream with open eyes, to make it possible." Churchill was a dreamer of the day. He lived his vision of victory every waking moment. With incredible physical and mental stamina, he led his nation and its allies against the Nazi wolf, the Italian jackal, and Japanese wolverine.

When I set out on this journey of discovery a lifetime ago, I had no idea that Churchill would be more than a passing interest. Sourced by a curiosity beginning on the day he died, I wondered, "Who was he?" The more I read about him, largely in his own words, I found his example offered numerous lessons and practices worth following. In both war and peace, I road tested many of these in demanding leadership positions. Vision, courage, and determination were valid then and offer leaders today a similar process for overcoming challenges of great consequence.

My motivation for writing this book was to help people and organizations step into the world of possibilities, especially those who want to be more, do more, and have more. A domain of boundless opportunities stands before you. Let vision, courage, and determination become familiar tools in your hands.

By using the Churchill factors, you will experience a richer, fuller, more productive life. May your organization push the envelope of achievement forward! You will only be limited by your collective imagination and will. Most important, you already possess the talents necessary to be successful. As John Buchan noted in his biography of King George V, *The King's Grace*, "The true task of leadership is not to put greatness into humanity but to elicit it since the greatness is already there."

Lead boldly and live victoriously!

"This is your victory!"
Winston S. Churchill

SELECT BIBLIOGRAPHY

Addison, Paul. *Churchill The Unexpected Hero*. Oxford: Oxford University Press, 2005.

Ashley, Maurice. *Churchill as Historian*. New York: Charles Scribner's Sons, 1968.

Beiriger, Eugene Edward. *Churchill, Munitions, and Mechanical Warfare: The Politics of Supply and Strategy*. New York: Peter Lang Publishing, 1997.

Bell, Christopher M. *Churchill and the Dardanelles*. Oxford: Oxford University Press, 2017.
------ *Churchill and Sea Power*. Oxford: Oxford University Press, 2012.

Berlin, Isaiah. *Mr. Churchill in 1940*. Boston: Houghton Mifflin Co., 1949.

Best, Geoffrey. *Churchill and War*. London: Hambledon and London, 2005

Bibesco, Marthe. *Sir Winston Churchill: Master of Courage*. London: Robert Hale Limited, 1957.

Brown, Anthony Cave. *Bodyguard of Lies*. New York: Harper & Row, 1975.

Bryant, Arthur. *The Turn of the Tide 1939-1943*. Based on the Diaries of F.M. Lord Alanbrooke. New York: Doubleday, 1957

Churchill, Sir Winston S., *A History of the English-Speaking People Volume 2: The New World*. New York: Dorset Press, 1956.
------ *Liberalism and the Social Problem*. London: Hodder and Stoughton, 1909.
------ *London to Ladysmith via Pretoria*. London: Longmans, Green, and Co., 1900.

------ *Lord Randolph Churchill*. London: Odhams Press Limited, 1951.

------ *Marlborough: His Life and Times Volume 2*. London: George G. Harrap & Co., 1934.

------ *My Early Life: A Roving Commission*. London: Thornton Butterworth Limited, 1930.

------ *Painting as a Pastime*. London: Odhams Books Limited, 1948.

------*The People's Rights*. New York: Taplinger Publishing Co., 1971.

------ *The Second World War Volume 1: The Gathering Storm*. Boston: Houghton Mifflin Company, 1948.

------ *The Second World War Volume 2: Their Finest Hour*. Boston: Houghton Mifflin Company, 1949.

------ *The Sinews of Peace: Post-War Speeches by Winston S. Churchill*. London: Cassell, 1948.

------ *The World Crisis Volume 2*. New York: Chas Scribner's Sons., 1923.

------ *The World Crisis Volume 4*. New York: Chas Scribner's Sons., 1927.

------ *Thoughts and Adventures*. London: Odhams Press Limited, 1932.

Colville, John. *The Fringes of Power: 10 Downing Street Diaries 1939-1955*. New York: W. W. Norton and Co., 1985.

------ *Foot-Prints in Time: Memories*. London: Collins, 1976.

------ *Winston Churchill and his Inner Circle*. New York: Wyndham Books, 1981.

Coombs, David with Churchill, Minnie. *Sir Winston Churchill: His Life and His Paintings*. Philadelphia: Running Press, 2003.

Gilbert, Sir Martin. *Churchill: A Life*. New York: Henry Holt and Co., 1991.

------ *Churchill and America*. New York: Free Press, 2005.

------ *Churchill and the Jews: A Lifelong Friendship*. New York: Henry Holt and Co., 2007.

------ *In Search of Churchill: A Historian's Journey*. New York: John Wiley and Sons, 1994.

------ *Winston S. Churchill Official Biography Volume 4: The Stricken World 1916-1922*. Boston: Houghton Mifflin Co., 1975.

------ *Winston S. Churchill Companion Volume 4, Part I, January 1917-June 1919*. Boston: Houghton Mifflin Co., 1977.

------ *Winston S. Churchill Official Biography Volume 6: Finest Hour 1939-1941*. Boston: Houghton Mifflin Co., 1983.

------ *Winston S. Churchill Official Biography Volume 7: Road to Victory 1941-1945*. Boston: Houghton Mifflin Co., 1986.

------ *Winston Churchill: The Wilderness Years*. Boston: Houghton Mifflin Co., 1982.

------ *Winston Churchill's War Leadership*. New York: Vintage Books, 2003.

Deming, W. Edwards. *Out of the Crisis*. Cambridge: Massachusetts Institute of Technology Center for Advanced Engineering Study, 1986.

D'Este Carlo. *Warlord: A Life of Winston Churchill at War—1874-1945*. New York: HarperCollins Publishers, 2008.

Gardner, John W. *On Leadership*. New York: Free Press, 1990.

Hayward, Steven F. *Churchill on Leadership: Executive Success in the Face of Adversity*. Rocklin: Forum, 1997.

------ *Greatness: Reagan, Churchill, and the Making of Extraordinary Leaders*. New York: Crown Forum, 2005.

Humes, James C. *The Sir Winston Method: The Five Secrets of Speaking the Language of Leadership*. New York: William Morrow and Co., 1991.

James, Robert Rhodes, editor. *Churchill Speaks 1897-1963: Collected Speeches in War & Peace*. New York: Barnes & Noble Books, 1998.

Jamison, Kay Redfield. *Exuberance: The Passion for Life*. New York: Alfred A. Knopf, 2004.

Jenkins, Roy. *Churchill: A Biography*. New York: Farrar, Straus, and Giroux, 2001.

Keegan, John. *Winston Churchill*. New York: Viking Book, 2002.

Kimball, Warren F, editor. *Churchill and Roosevelt: The Complete Correspondence Volume 1—Alliance Emerging*. Princeton: Princeton University Press, 1984.
------ *Forged in War: Roosevelt, Churchill, and the Second World War*. New York: William Morrow & Co., 1997.

Korda, Michael. *Alone: Britain, Churchill, and Dunkirk: Defeat into Victory*. New York: Liveright Publishing, 2017.

Kryske, Larry. *The Churchill Factors: Creating Your Finest Hour*. Victoria: Trafford Publishing, 2000.
------ *Ready, BEGIN! Practical Strategies for Cultivating Courage*. Victoria: Trafford Publishing, 2008.

Kryske, Naomi. *The Witness: A Novel*. Nashville: Dunham Books, 2012.
------ *The Mission: A Novel*. Nashville: Dunham Books, 2015.

Langworth, Richard, editor. *Churchill by Himself: The Definitive Collection of Quotations*. New York: Public Affairs, 2008.

Lavery, Brian. *Churchill Goes to War: Winston's Wartime Journeys*. London: Conway, 2008.

Lukacs, John. *Churchill: Visionary, Statesman, Historian*. New Haven; Yale University Press, 2002.
------ *Five Days in London May, 1940*. New Haven: Yale University Press, 1999.

Marder, Arthur J. *From Dreadnought to Scapa Flow Volume 2; The War Years to the Eve of Jutland—1914-1916*. Oxford: Oxford University Press, 1965.

Manchester, William. *The Last Lion Winston S. Churchill: Visions of Glory, 1874-1932*. Boston: Little, Brown and Co., 1983
------ *The Last Lion Winston S. Churchill: Alone, 1932-1940*. Boston: Little, Brown and Co., 1988.

Manchester, William and Reid, Paul. *The Last Lion Winston S. Churchill: Defender of the Realm, 1940-1965*. Boston: Little, Brown and Co., 2012.

Meacham, John. *Franklin and Winston: An Intimate Portrait of an Epic Friendship*. New York: Random House, 2003.

Millard, Candice. *Hero of the Empire: The Boer War, A Daring Escape, and the Making of Winston Churchill*. New York: Doubleday, 2016.

Nixon, Richard. *Leaders: Profiles and Reminiscences of Men Who Have Shaped the Modern World*. New York: Warner Books, 1982.

Olson, Lynne. *Troublesome Young Men: The Rebels Who Brought Churchill to Power and Helped Save England*. New York: Farrar, Straus, and Giroux. 2007.

Parker, R. A. C. editor. *Winston Churchill: Studies in Statesmanship*. London: Brassey's, 1995.

Parrish, Thomas. *To Keep the British Isles Afloat: FDR's Men in Churchill's London, 1941*. New York: HarperCollins, 2009.

Pawle, Gerald. *The War and Colonel Warden*. London: George G. Harrap & Co. 1963

Phillips, Donald T. *Lincoln on Leadership for Today: Abraham Lincoln's Approach to 21st-Century Issues*. Boston: Houghton Mifflin Harcourt, 2017.

Purnell, Sonia. *Clementine: The Life of Mrs. Winston Churchill*. New York: Viking, 2015.

Rankin, Nicholas. *Churchill's Wizards: The British Genius for Deception, 1914-1945*. London: Faber and Faber, 2008.

Reynolds, David. *In Command of History: Churchill Fighting and Writing the Second World War*. London: Penguin Books, 2005.

Roberts, Andrew. *Eminent Churchillians*. London: Phoenix, 1994. ------ *Hitler & Churchill: The Secrets of Leadership*. London: Weidenfeld & Nicolson, 2003.

Russell, Douglas S. *Winston Churchill Soldier: The Military Life of a Gentleman at War*. London: Brassey's, 2005.

Sandys, Celia. *Churchill Wanted Dead or Alive*. New York: Carroll & Graf Publishers, 1999.

Sandys, Celia and Littman, Jonathan. *We Shall Not Fail: The Inspiring Leadership of Winston Churchill*. New York: Portfolio. 2003.

Shelden, Michael. *Young Titan: The Making of Winston Churchill*. New York: Simon & Schuster, 2013.

Soames, Mary. *Winston Churchill His Life as a Painter: A Memoir by His Daughter*. London: Collins, 1990.

Toye, Richard. *Churchill's Empire: The World that Made Him and the World He Made*. New York: Henry Holt & Co., 2010.

Wheeler-Bennett, Sir John, editor. *Action this Day: Working with Churchill*. New York: St. Martin's Press, 1969.

ACKNOWLEDGEMENTS

Winston Churchill indicated that "a fanatic is one who can't change his mind and won't change the subject." By definition, I have been a fanatic about Churchill for all my adult life.

I have been blessed by the contributions of many generous, knowledgeable, and conscientious friends. Some contributed countless hours while others offered a word of encouragement at just the right moment. Without their dedicated help, this book would not be possible.

I sincerely appreciate the assistance from: RADM Curtis A. Kemp, CDR Bruce Wolven (CANOA), Donald T. Phillips, RADM Scott Hebner, Congressman Gene Taylor, Paul Kryske, Richard H. Knight, Jr., Thomas F. Gede, Jeffrey D. Gottlieb, Dr. David Freeman, CAPT Marc Helgeson, Kenneth Fielding Morehead, Nan Towsley, Dr. James E. Auer, Paul M. Gottlieb, Richard Langworth, CAPT H. Wyman Howard, Mark Randolph Towsley, CAPT W. Dallas Bethea (CANOA), CAPT Robert D. Moser, John Henry King, Cheryl Servais, Julie Tabor, Kyle Kryske, Joni McPherson, Dr. Chris Terrill, Rev. Larry N. Ramsey, Gene Wismer, and Master Chief Musician Jay A. Piper. For my Churchillian friends, KBO. For my Navy shipmates, AD 28. For my friends who are believers, Ephesians 3:16-19.

My parents, Leon and Annette (may she rest in peace), have aided and abetted me in my Churchill habit.

I have also been privileged to have been helped by three generations of Churchills over the years. Lady Soames (Mary Churchill, Churchill's youngest daughter) in 1990 shared with me Churchill's favorite brand of cognac and answered other questions. Winston S. Churchill, MP, Churchill's grandson, kindly told me about the International Society in 1987. And through the ICS, I met my future wife. Randolph S. Churchill, Sir Winston's great-grandson, graciously shared his hospitality and time with my wife and me in 2013.

The International Churchill Society has exposed me to kindred spirits, Churchillians, many of whom have become stalwart friends. Their quarterly journal, *Finest Hour*, is a great resource about all things Churchill. ICS also has a superb website, www.WinstonChurchill.org.

I would be remiss if I did not single out my wife, Naomi, for assistance above and beyond the call of duty. Her involvement with every facet of this book has been unconditional, considerable, and extraordinary! "Awesome" is too insignificant a word to describe her generous and loving contributions.

> *"But united, concentrated, combined,*
> *working together in true comradeship,*
> *there is no foe who can bar our path."*
> **Winston S. Churchill**

ABOUT THE AUTHOR

Commander Lawrence M. (Larry) Kryske, U.S. Navy (Ret.), develops victorious leaders who have vision, courage, and determination. He is a professional speaker, certified trainer, and facilitator who has over thirty-five years of worldwide success leading men and women and building unstoppable teams.

As a career naval officer, Larry drove warships for a living. In his first ship, he was involved in combat operations during the Vietnam War. He served ashore in Naval Intelligence in Japan, on the Chief of Naval Operations' staff in the Pentagon, and with the Defense Nuclear Agency. Larry was also the first commanding officer of U.S. Naval Station, Pascagoula, Mississippi, which was the Navy's newest, most technologically modern, environmentally clean base in the world.

He later served as a private school administrator and instructor, teaching courses on leadership (among other courses) for high school students at two schools.

Larry is president of Your Finest Hour Leadership Programs, a full-service leadership development business that he started in 1996. He speaks nationwide on leadership, teamwork, and innovation. He has given keynotes, conducted training seminars, and facilitated leadership retreats for over four hundred corporate, non-profit (trade associations), governmental, educational, and civic organizations in over fifty different industries.

Larry is a respected authority on the life and leadership of Winston Churchill. He served a three-year term on the Board of Directors of the International Churchill Society. He shared the speaking platform with Sir Martin Gilbert, Official Biographer of Sir Winston S. Churchill, at a Churchill Leadership Symposium on the Queen Mary in

2001. From 1999-2006, Larry presented his painting keynote presentation about Winston Churchill, *Creating Your Finest Hour*, to over 50,000 attendees.

He also authored three previous books about leadership and is a landscape oil painter.

Larry has a BA in Astronomy from the University of California at Los Angeles (UCLA) and an MS in Applied Science from the Naval Postgraduate School in Monterey, CA. He resides in Plano, Texas, with his wife, Naomi, a novelist.

Contact Larry at:
Larry@YourFinestHour.com

CPSIA information can be obtained
at www.ICGtesting.com
Printed in the USA
LVHW02s1525280118
564232LV00008B/13/P